Campaign

A Cartoon History of Bill Clinton's Race for the White House

Compiled and Edited by

Mary Ann Barton

and

Paul C. Barton

THE UNIVERSITY OF ARKANSAS PRESS

FAYETTEVILLE   1993

Manufactured in the United States of America

97 96 95 94 93 5 4 3 2 1

Designed by Gail Carter

The paper used in this publication meets the minimum requirements of the American National Standard for Permanence of Paper for Printed Library Materials Z39.48-1984. ♾

Library of Congress Cataloging-in-Publication Data

Campaign: a cartoon history of Bill Clinton's race for the White House / compiled and edited by Mary Ann Barton and Paul C. Barton.
p. cm.
ISBN 1-55728-289-7
1. Presidents—United States—Election—1992—Caricatures and cartoons. 2. Clinton, Bill, 1946- —Caricatures and cartoons. 3. United States—Politics and government—1989-1993—Caricatures and cartoons. 4. American wit and humor, Pictorial. I. Barton, Mary Ann, 1959- . II. Barton, Paul C., 1957- .
E884.C36 1993
973.929'092—dc20 93-2984
CIP

To our parents

Acknowledgments

Campaign would not have been possible without the work of inspired cartoonists from across the nation. We want to thank them (and their spouses, assistants, editors, and syndicates) for taking the time—by phone, FAX, or Federal Express—to give us their permission to reprint and wish we could have included every drawing.

We are grateful for the direction we received from the University of Arkansas Press, especially the gentle prodding from editor Debbie Bowen, as well as help from John Coghlan, production manager, and Beth Garrett, marketing manager.

We would also like to thank the helpful people at the Eudora Welty Library in Jackson, Mississippi.

Contents

Introduction   *ix*

Isn't Anyone Going to Get In?   *2*

Elvis   *12*

Tabloid Tales   *16*

The Draft   *26*

The Comeback Kid   *38*

Hillary   *42*

The Bubba Factor   *50*

JFK   *52*

Inhale   *54*

Perotmania   *58*

Once More into the Breach   *76*

Perot's Out   *98*

The Convention   *106*

Back into the Fray   *118*

Family Values   *128*

The Debate on Debates   *142*

Perot: He's Back . . .   *152*

Hitting the Television Trail   *160*

Moscow   *174*

The Final Days   *182*

And the Rest Is History   *202*

Introduction

For political cartoonists, Bill Clinton's 1992 campaign for the presidency offered a target-rich environment. The process that made the twelve-year Arkansas governor our president forced him to hurdle charges of marital infidelity, draft dodging, and pot smoking, and to sing a few bars of Elvis hits along the way.

He also played the sax (while wearing sunglasses) on "The Arsenio Hall Show," tangled with talk-show hosts, and defended his wife as a homemaker.

It was a year of bus trips and cookie recipes, 1-800 telephone numbers, politics on MTV, spelling contests, and a television character named Murphy Brown, who helped highlight the so-called family-values issue.

Clinton was an enigma to the nation for most of the year as he battled caricatures that saw him sometimes as Bubba and other times as Slick Willie, the smooth-talking car salesman who promised everything to all.

Clinton was probably most accurately portrayed, however, as the intrepid candidate who trudged through swamps where lesser politicians would have sunk. A cartoon that perhaps best sums up the year is one in which a Frankenstein-like Clinton, punctured by spears, swords, and arrows, continues to advance to the Democratic nomination with an ax in his head.

In short, 1992 was a bouillabaisse of eccentric characters and events. President Bush probably said it well enough when he termed the campaign year "weird" and "strange."

Despite all of its oddities, however, it was also a deadly serious campaign for American voters who appeared to have developed a revived interest in issues and voting, in part out of a concern that America was losing its way in a new and uncertain world. *Newsweek* magazine called 1992 the "year of living seriously." Highlighting it was concern about a sluggish economy and a seemingly endless procession of layoff announcements.

Against this backdrop, the nation's best political cartoonists went to work lampooning Clinton and his fellow candidates in a variety of ways. The attraction of political cartoons is that they can capture issues and personalities with an immediacy that prose rarely achieves. This they had no problem doing in 1992.

Campaign is an attempt to reflect the flavor of the Clinton race as captured by these cartoonists. We hope you can sit back and enjoy the images you see here, reliving some of the issues from a campaign that, as many observers said, could easily have been scripted in Hollywood. Perhaps, too, you will gain new insight into the American political process from many of the country's finest political commentators.

Paul C. Barton
December 1992
Jackson, Mississippi

Campaign

Isn't Anyone Going to Get In?

Rob Rogers

With President Bush's approval ratings remaining high throughout most of 1991, Democrats were reluctant to step forward to challenge him. A number of big names, ranging from Jay Rockefeller to Bill Bradley to Richard Gephardt, decided not to run, clearing a path for Gov. Bill Clinton of Arkansas.

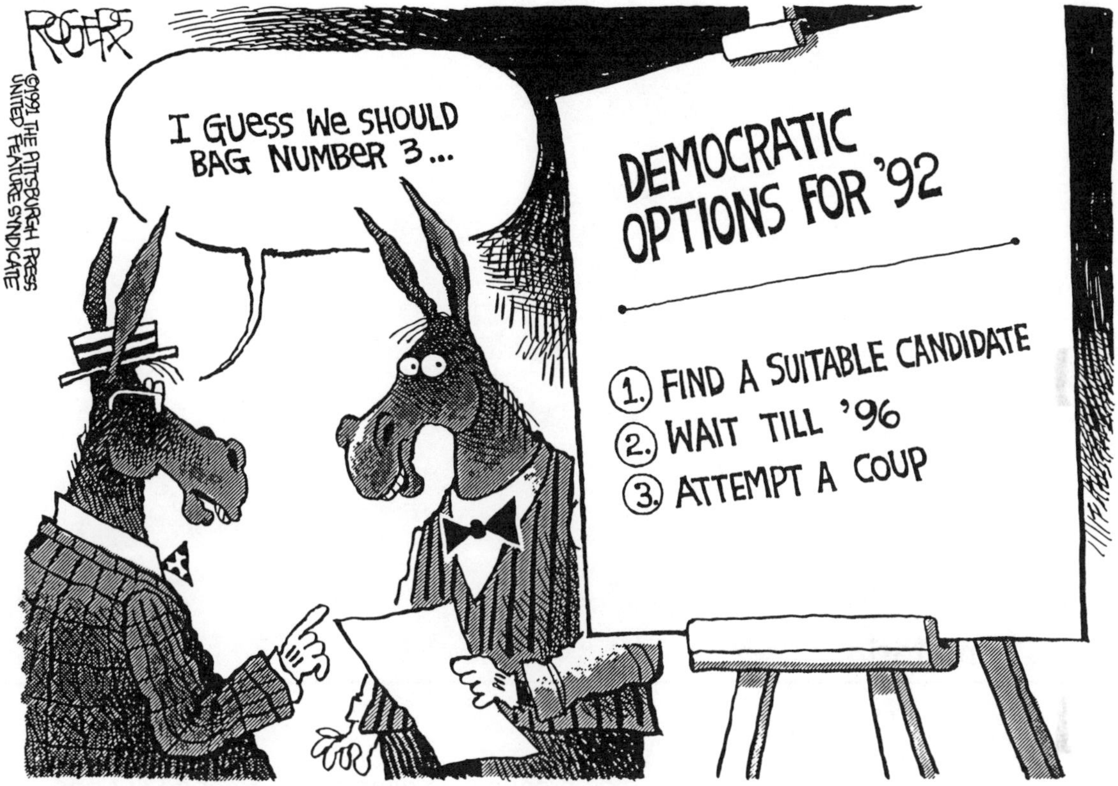
ROGERS
©1991 THE PITTSBURGH PRESS
UNITED FEATURE SYNDICATE
I GUESS WE SHOULD BAG NUMBER 3...
DEMOCRATIC OPTIONS FOR '92
1. FIND A SUITABLE CANDIDATE
2. WAIT TILL '96
3. ATTEMPT A COUP

Jim Morin

Party officials got nervous as prospective candidates dropped out one by one.

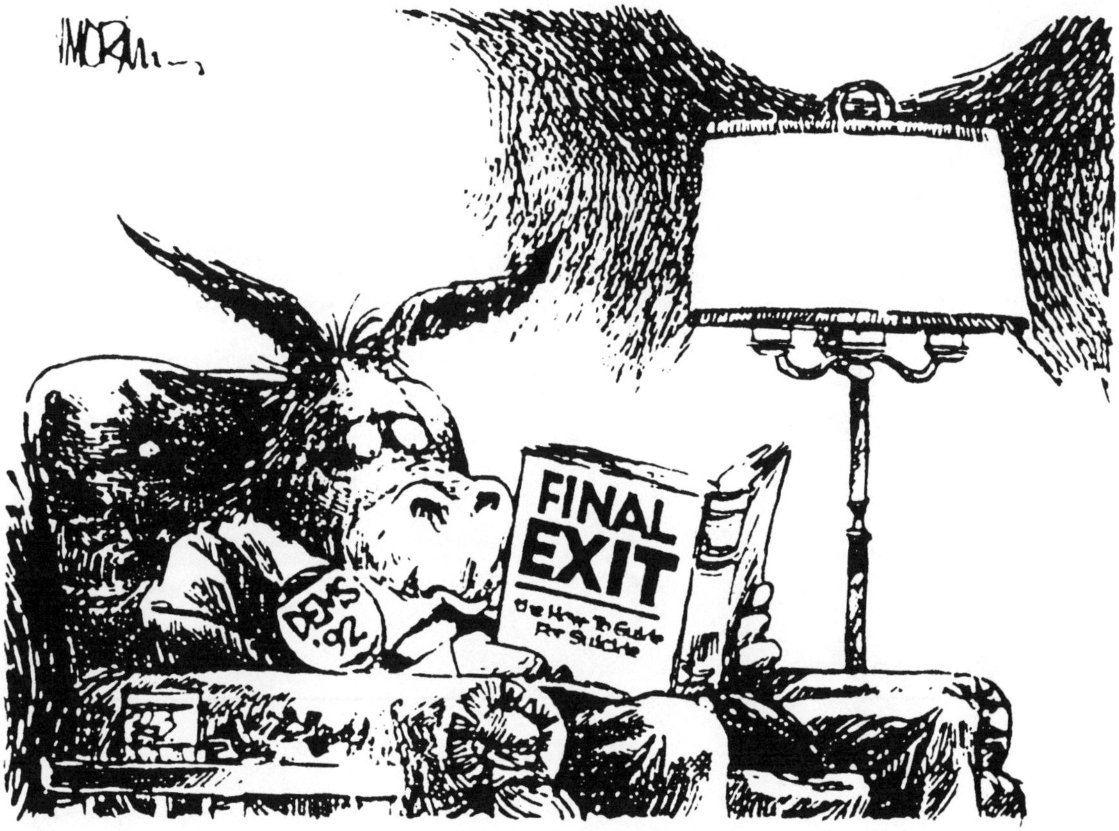
FINAL
EXIT

George Fisher

Throughout most of 1991, a seemingly endless drama played itself out in Little Rock, as Clinton agonized over whether to run for president. He made it official October 3.

Courtesy of George Fisher and the *Arkansas Democrat-Gazette*

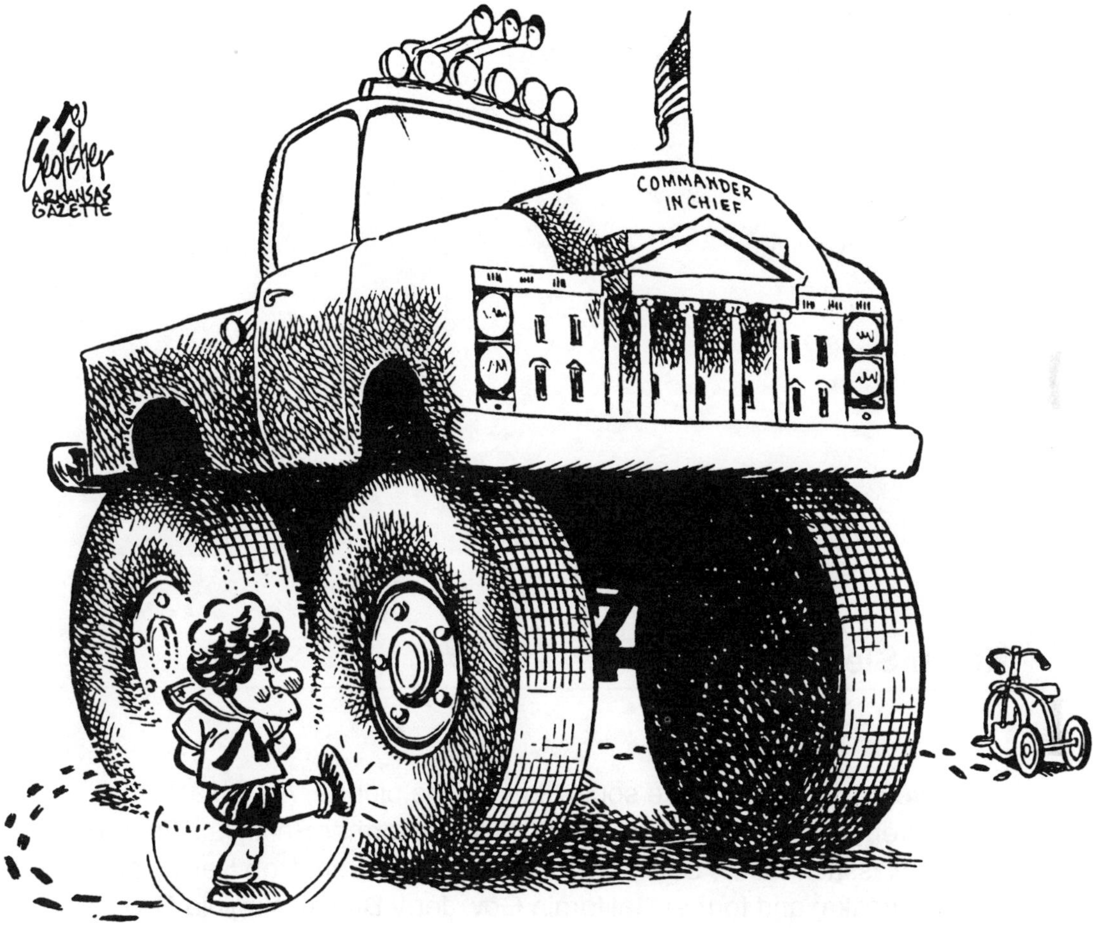

ARKANSAS GAZETTE
COMMANDER IN CHIEF

Kevin Siers

Eventually, a few brave souls did take the plunge, Arkansas's governor among them. The field included former Sen. Paul Tsongas of Massachusetts; Sen. Tom Harkin of Iowa; Sen. Bob Kerrey of Nebraska; and former California Gov. Jerry Brown. Virginia Gov. Doug Wilder bowed out in January.

Courtesy of Kevin Siers and *The Charlotte Observer*

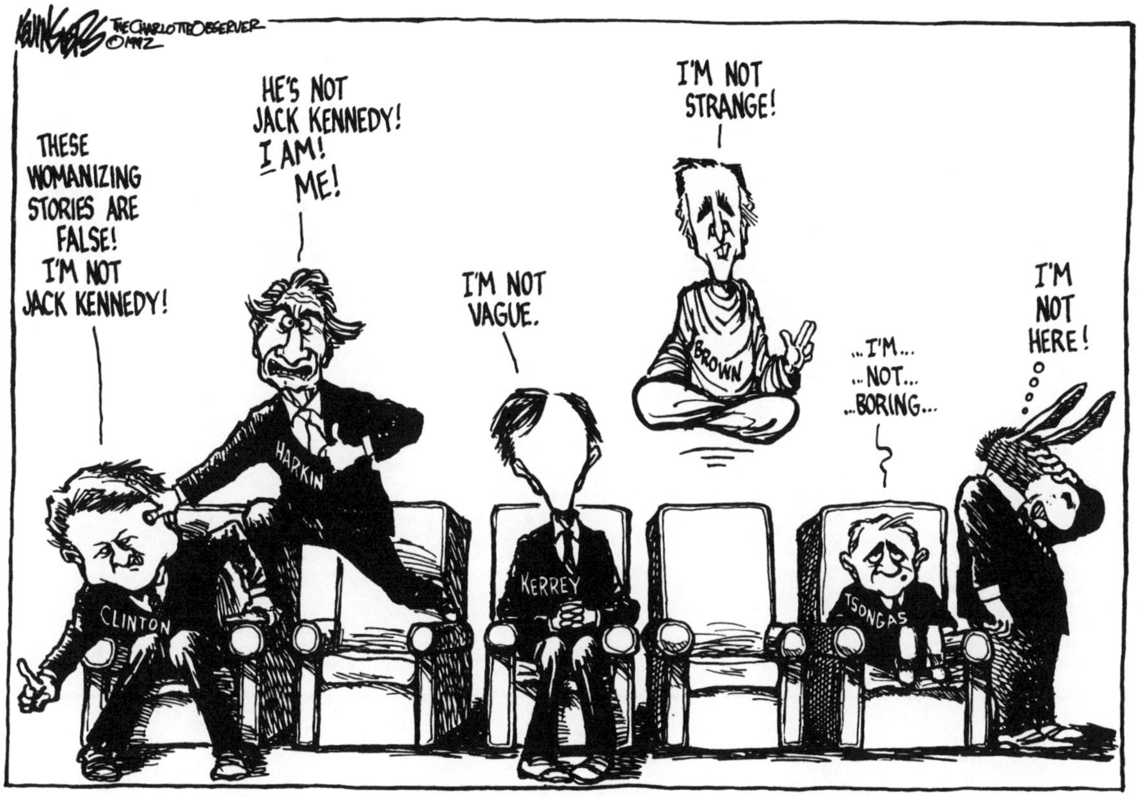
THE CHARLOTTE OBSERVER ©1992
THESE WOMANIZING STORIES ARE FALSE! I'M NOT JACK KENNEDY!
HE'S NOT JACK KENNEDY! I AM! ME!
I'M NOT VAGUE.
I'M NOT STRANGE!
...I'M... ...NOT... ...BORING...
I'M NOT HERE!
CLINTON
HARKIN
KERREY
BROWN
TSONGAS

John Branch

Soon after the campaign got underway, Clinton was tagged the front-runner; but past elections had shown that that wasn't always a good omen.

John Branch, *San Antonio Express-News*

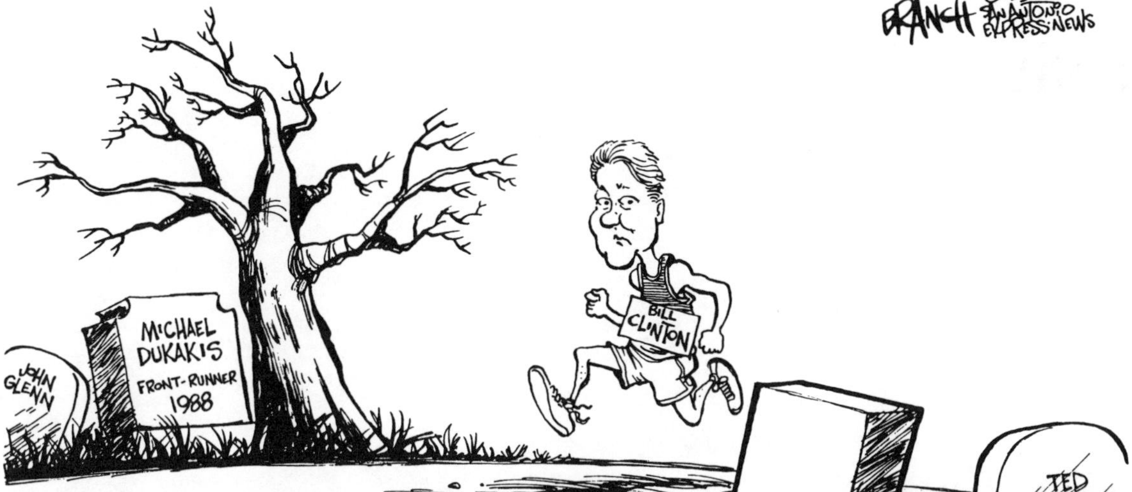
BRANCH ©1992 SAN ANTONIO EXPRESS-NEWS
JOHN GLENN
MICHAEL DUKAKIS
FRONT-RUNNER
1988
BILL CLINTON
TED KENNEDY
FRONT-RUNNER
1980
WALTER MONDALE
FRONT-RUNNER
1984
GARY HART
FRONT-RUNNER

Elvis

Don Wright

The panoply of Democratic candidates ranged from the mild-mannered Tsongas to Clinton, dubbed "Elvis" by the traveling press.

Don Wright, *The Palm Beach Post*

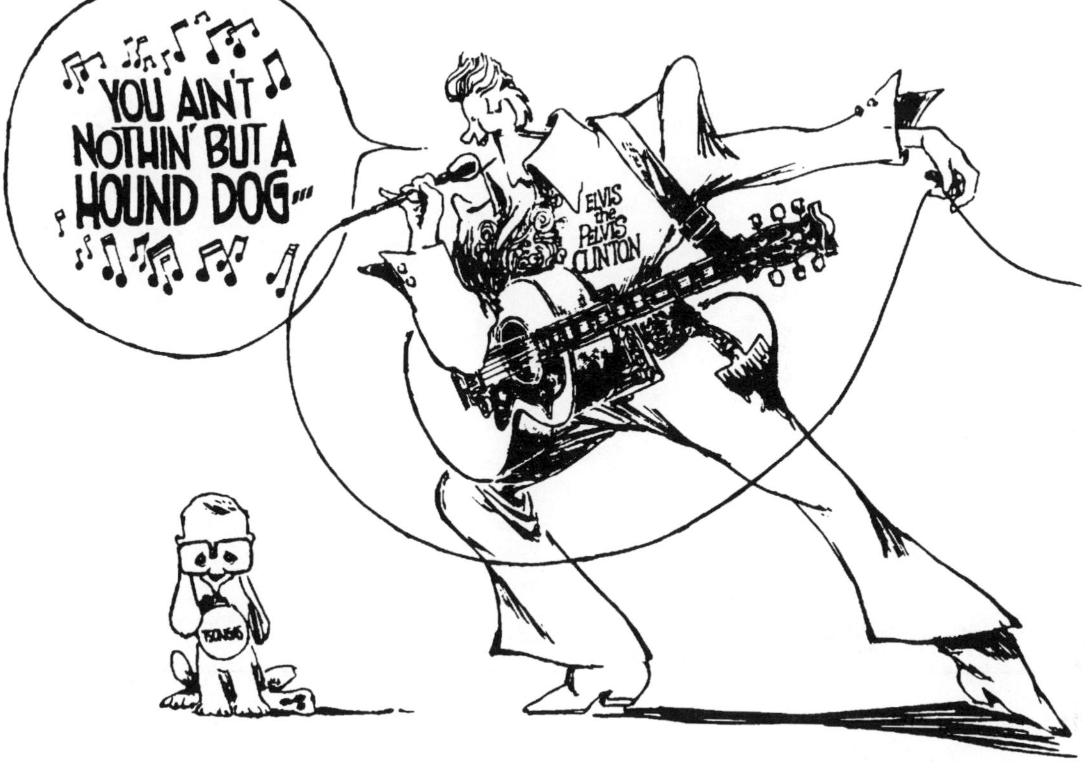
YOU AIN'T NOTHIN' BUT A HOUND DOG...
ELVIS the PELVIS CLINTON

Tom Toles

The Elvis theme continued throughout the year. When the fall campaign rolled around, Bush warned, "Americans will be checking into the Heartbreak Hotel."

Tom Toles in *The Buffalo News*

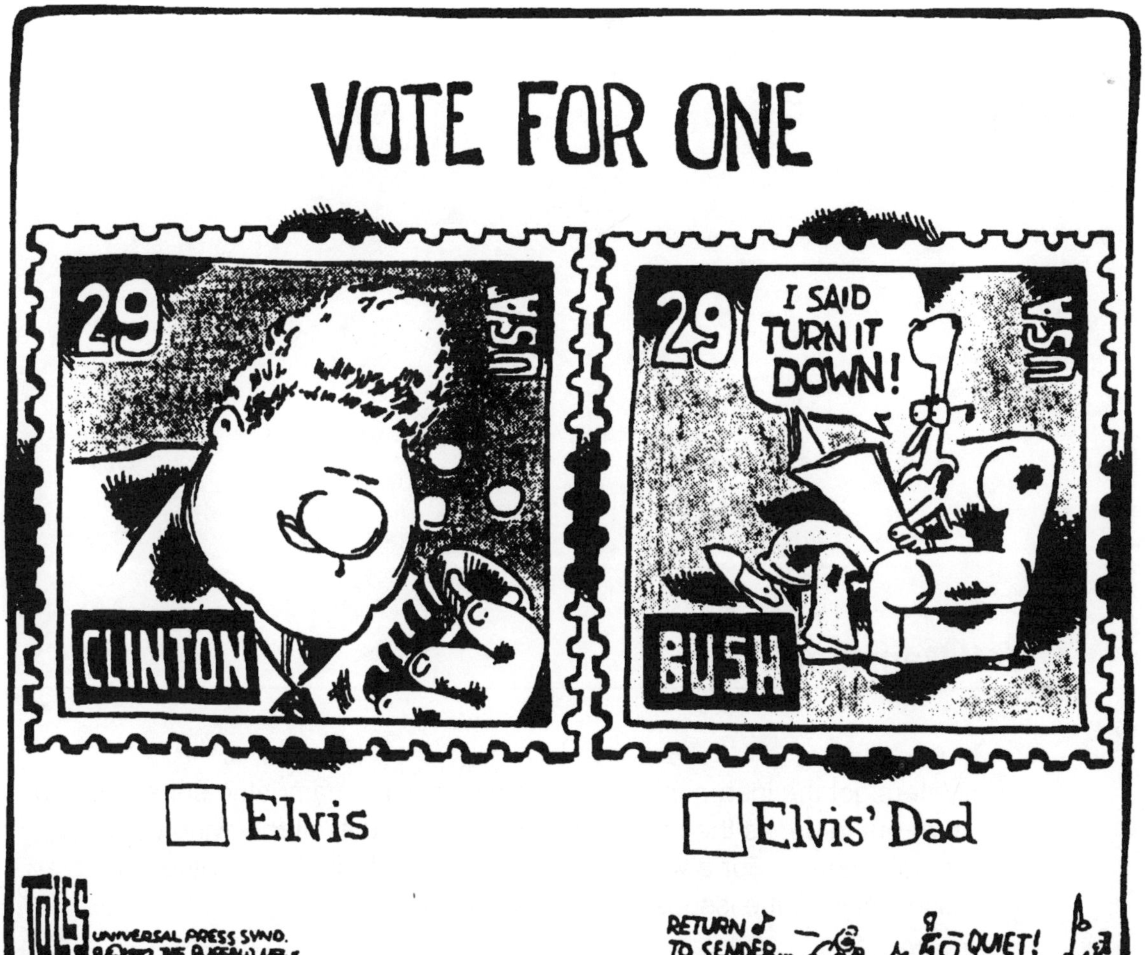
VOTE FOR ONE
29
USA
CLINTON
29
USA
I SAID TURN IT DOWN!
BUSH
Elvis
Elvis' Dad
TOLES
UNIVERSAL PRESS SYND.
© 1992 THE BUFFALO NEWS
RETURN TO SENDER...
QUIET!

Tabloid Tales

Jeff Danziger

Voters got the idea early on just how wacky the campaign season could turn out to be, as the mainstream media found itself following up on tabloid stories. For a while, the sensational tab stories smothered discussion of the issues.

Danziger in *The Christian Science Monitor* ©1992 TCSPS

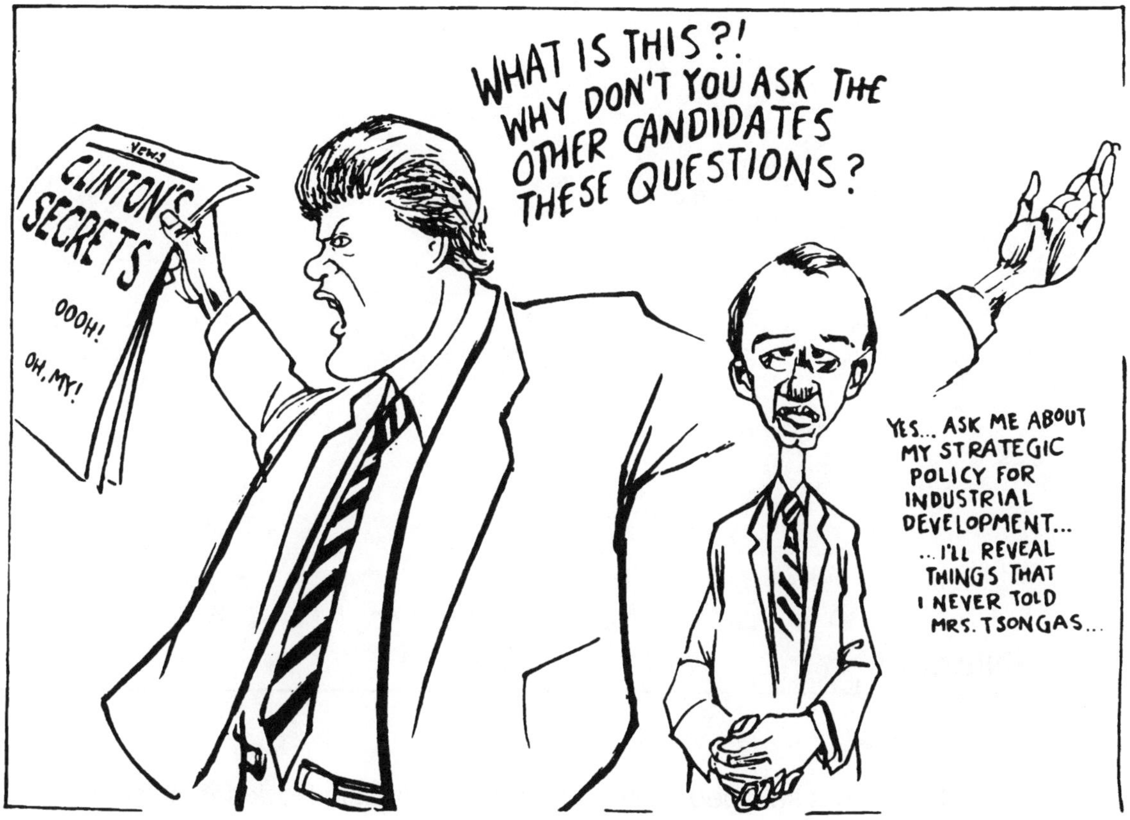
WHAT IS THIS?!
WHY DON'T YOU ASK THE OTHER CANDIDATES THESE QUESTIONS?
NEWS
CLINTON'S SECRETS
OOOH!
OH, MY!
YES... ASK ME ABOUT MY STRATEGIC POLICY FOR INDUSTRIAL DEVELOPMENT...
...I'LL REVEAL THINGS THAT I NEVER TOLD MRS. TSONGAS...

Oliphant

Clinton was savaged early, as journalists hit Little Rock searching for evidence of rumored womanizing.

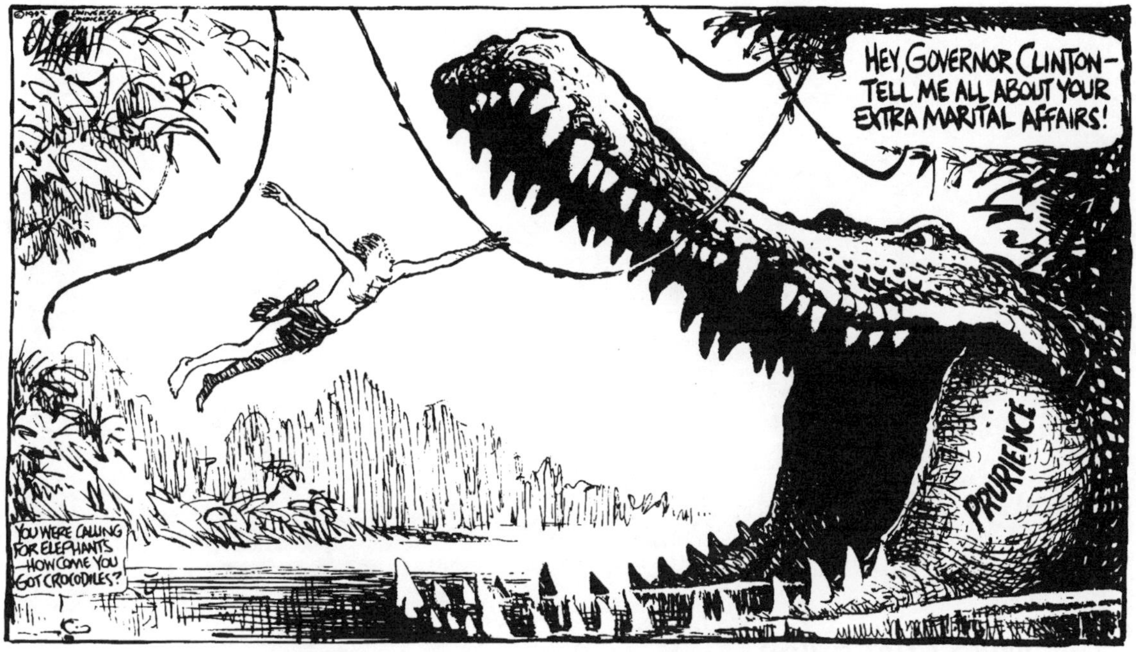
HEY, GOVERNOR CLINTON – TELL ME ALL ABOUT YOUR EXTRA MARITAL AFFAIRS!
PRURIENCE
YOU WERE CALLING FOR ELEPHANTS —HOW COME YOU GOT CROCODILES?
OLIPHANT

Mike Luckovich

The tabloids offered cash for trash. Former lounge singer and TV reporter Gennifer Flowers stepped forward to say she'd had a twelve-year affair with Governor Clinton.

Creators Syndicate

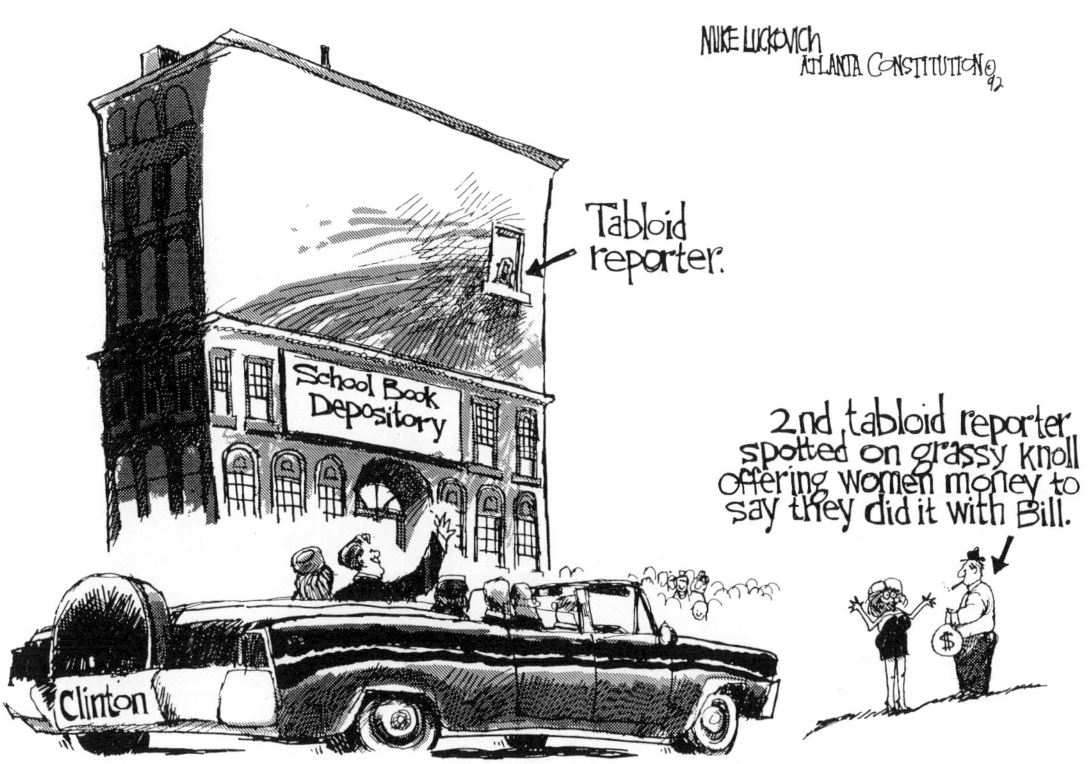
MIKE LUCKOVICH
ATLANTA CONSTITUTION © 92
Tabloid reporter.
School Book Depository
2nd tabloid reporter spotted on grassy knoll offering women money to say they did it with Bill.
Clinton
$

Doug Marlette

Soon the question became whether stories in the tabs were worthy of being repeated by the mainstream press.

Creators Syndicate

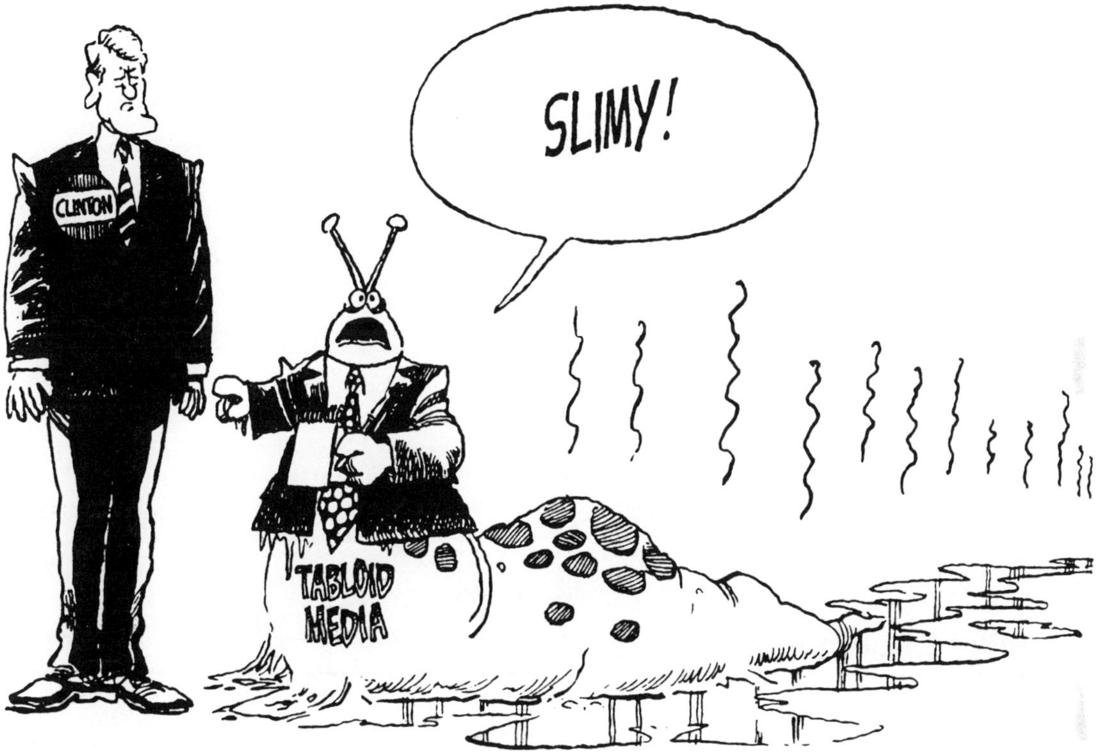
SLIMY!
CLINTON
TABLOID MEDIA

Mike Luckovich

It was an unprecedented focus on personal issues that raised questions about the focus of campaign coverage.

Creators Syndicate

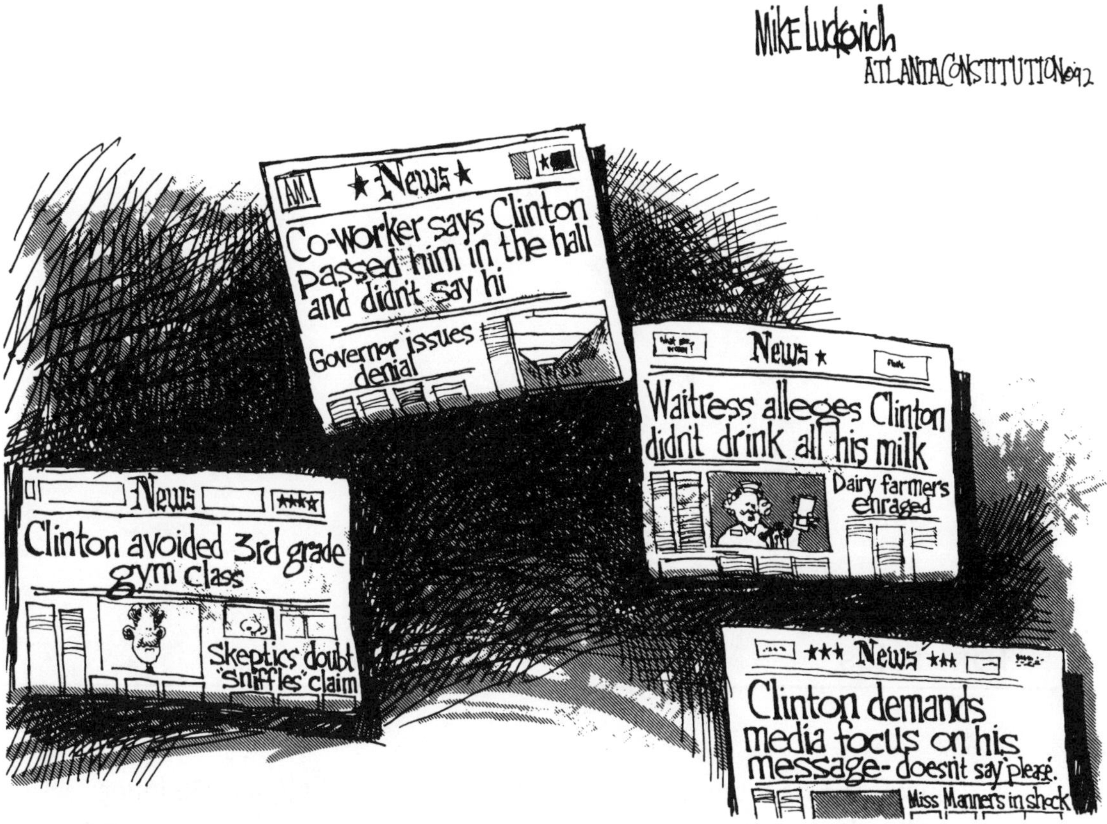
Mike Luckovich
ATLANTA CONSTITUTION ©92
News
Co-worker says Clinton passed him in the hall and didn't say hi
Governor issues denial
News
Waitress alleges Clinton didn't drink all his milk
Dairy farmers enraged
News
Clinton avoided 3rd grade gym class
Skeptics doubt "sniffles" claim
News
Clinton demands media focus on his message- doesn't say 'please'.
Miss Manners in shock

The Draft

Tom Toles

Just when he thought he had personal issues licked, a 1969 letter written by the then twenty-three-year-old Clinton surfaced, thanking Col. Eugene Holmes for saving him from the draft. The manner in which Clinton skirted military service now became a campaign issue.

Tom Toles in *The Buffalo News*

Deferral: a postponement to a later date.
DRAFT ISSUE
DRAFT ISSUE
DRAFT ISSUE
Pvt. Clinton
DRAFT ISSUE
DRAFT ISSUE
DRAFT ISSUE
DRAFT ISSUE
DRAFT ISSUE
DRAFT ISSUE
DRAFT ISSUE
1992
POST-NON-COMBAT STRESS SYNDROME
TOLES
©1992 THE BUFFALO NEWS

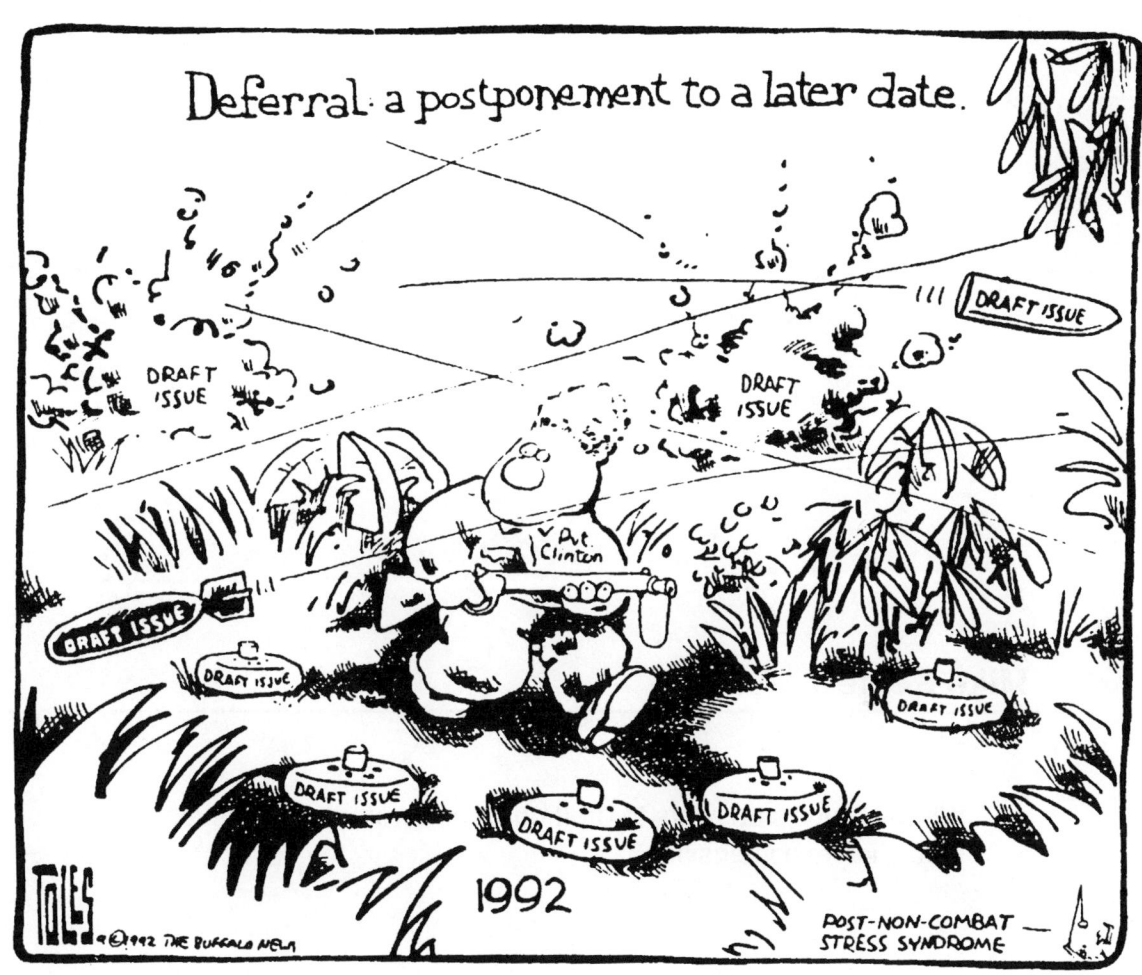

Mike Keefe

When Clinton's answers to draft questions were deemed evasive, media interest intensified.

Mike Keefe, *The Denver Post*

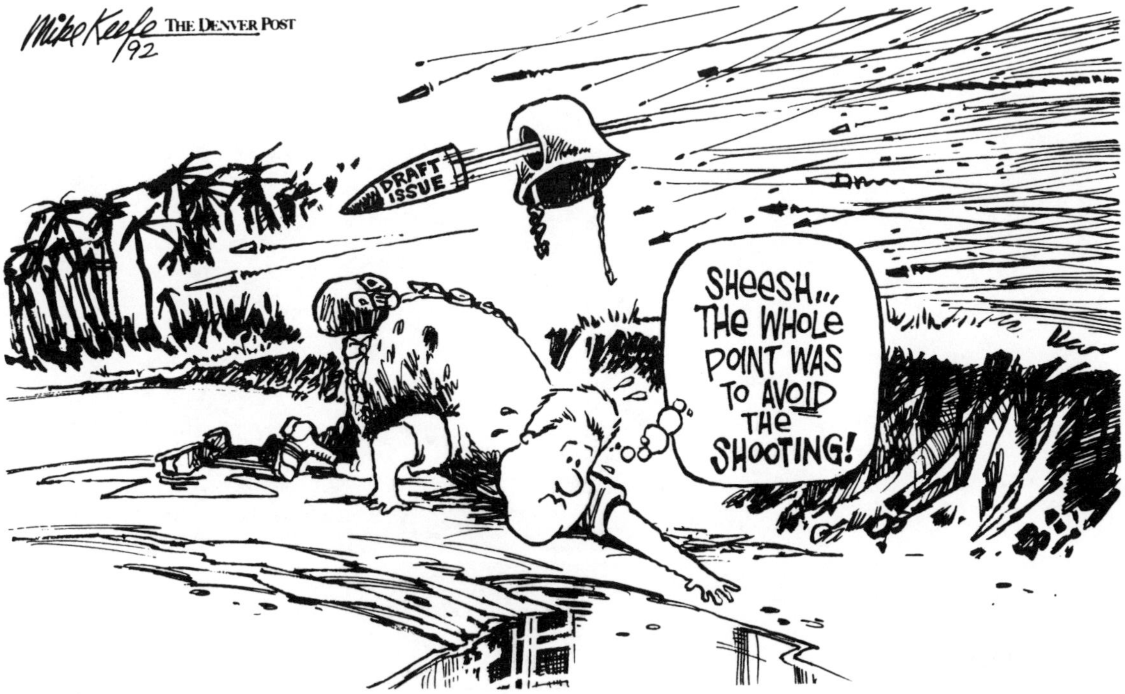
Mike Keefe THE DENVER POST
/92
DRAFT ISSUE
SHEESH... THE WHOLE POINT WAS TO AVOID THE SHOOTING!

Dunagin

The draft issue sparked debate on the op-ed pages of the nation's newspapers.

Courtesy of *The Orlando Sentinel* and North America Syndicate, Inc.

VETS
OF
ARMED
FORCES

10-7

"MAYBE HE THOUGHT HE COULD BETTER SERVE HIS COUNTRY BY LIVING TO BECOME PRESIDENT."

Mike Luckovich

The issue refused to die, as contradictions and Clinton's draft explanation continued to emerge.

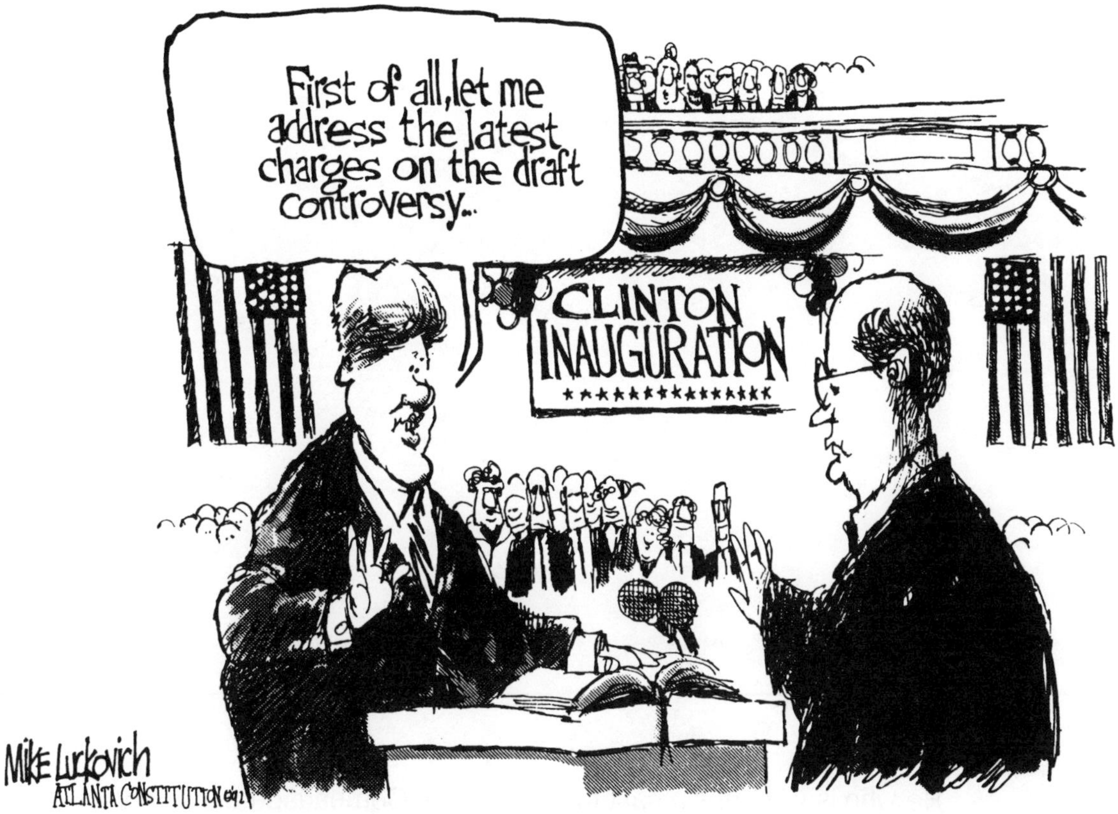
First of all, let me address the latest charges on the draft controversy...
CLINTON INAUGURATION
MIKE LUCKOVICH
ATLANTA CONSTITUTION

Conrad

He who is without sin cast the first stone. Comparison of military records abounded.

Reprinted by permission: *The Los Angeles Times*

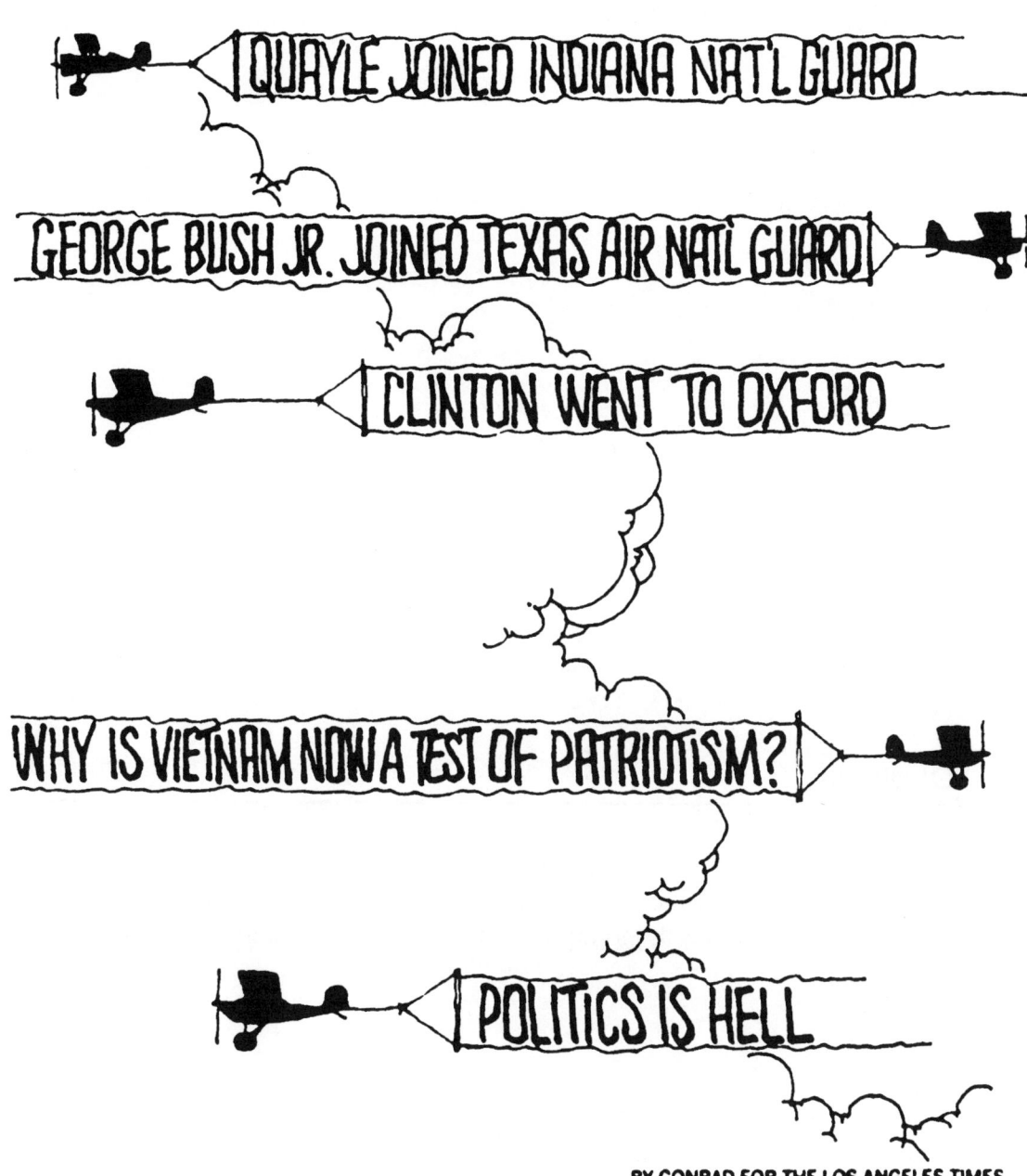

QUAYLE JOINED INDIANA NAT'L GUARD

GEORGE BUSH JR. JOINED TEXAS AIR NAT'L GUARD

CLINTON WENT TO OXFORD

WHY IS VIETNAM NOW A TEST OF PATRIOTISM?

POLITICS IS HELL

BY CONRAD FOR THE LOS ANGELES TIMES

WAR STORIES

Oliphant

To many, what Clinton had done twenty-three years before seemed trivial compared with the burning issues facing the nation in 1992.

CARE
NATIONAL DEBT
UNEMPLOYMENT
AND HOW YOU PROLONGED IT?

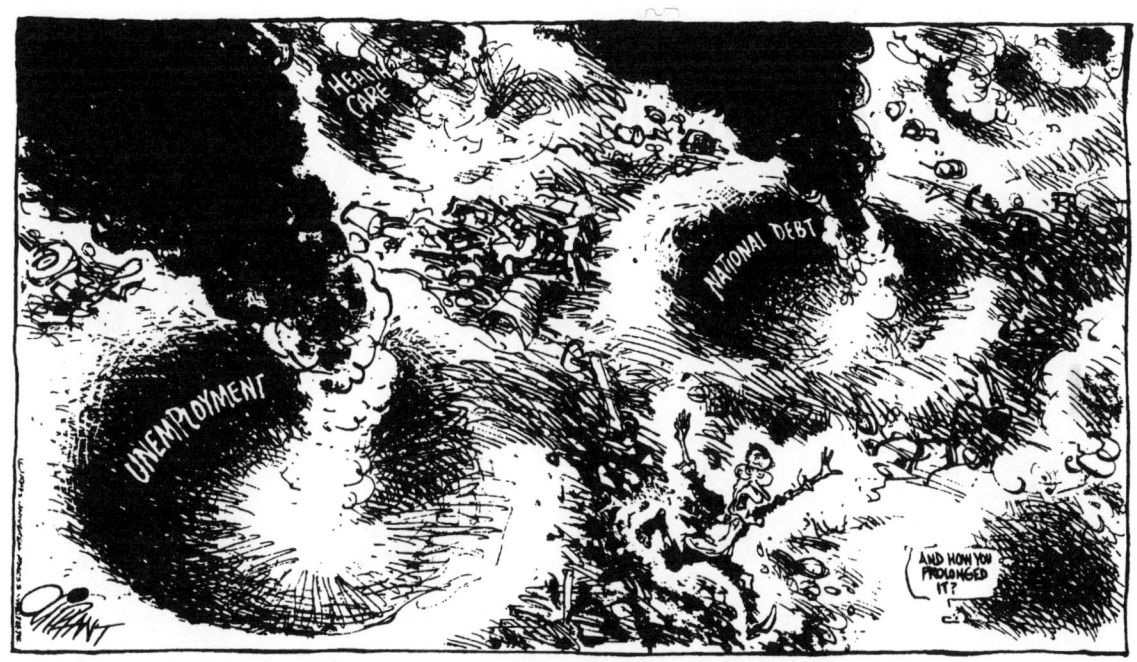

'WAIT! LET'S TALK ABOUT THE VIETNAM WAR!'

The Comeback Kid

Jack Ohman

After battling stories about alleged extramarital affairs and draft evasion, Clinton rallied to a second-place finish in the New Hampshire primary, good enough to keep his campaign alive. Meanwhile, Pat Buchanan exposed weaknesses in President Bush's support by getting close to 40 percent of the vote.

The Oregonian. Tribune Media Services

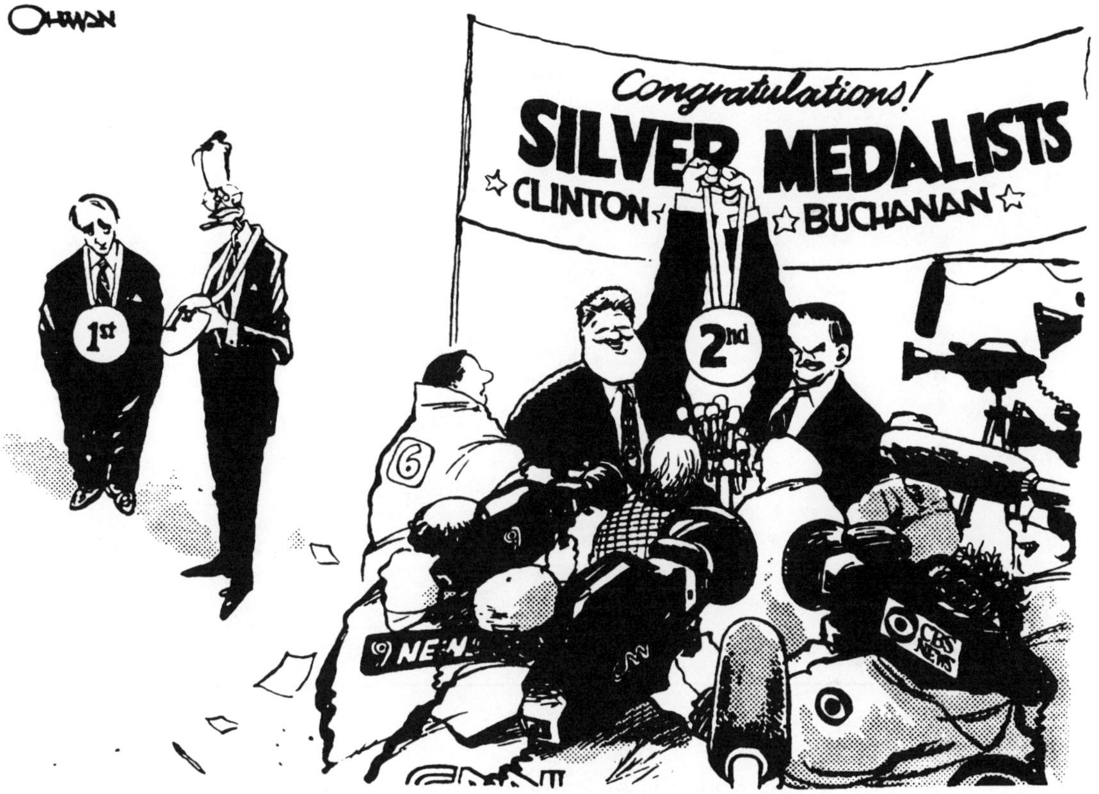
OHMAN
Congratulations!
SILVER MEDALISTS
CLINTON
BUCHANAN
1st
2nd
6
NEWS
CBS NEWS

Tom Toles

In politics, perception is everything. That a once-faltering Clinton
campaign came back to finish second with 25 percent of the vote was
seen as a major accomplishment for the governor. Clinton dubbed
himself "The Comeback Kid."

Tom Toles in *The Buffalo News*

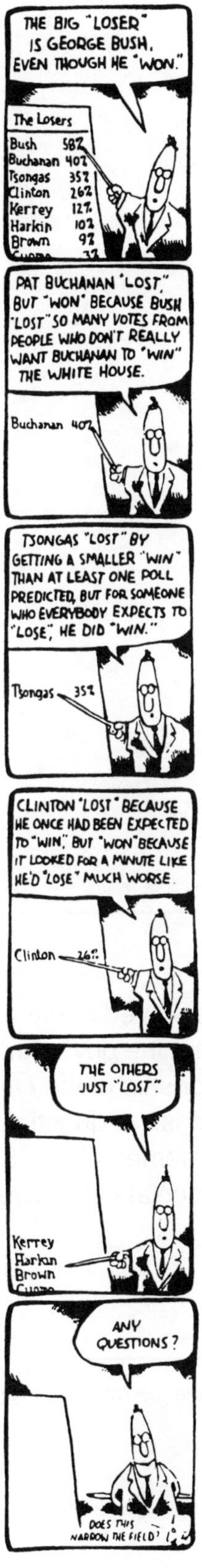
THE BIG "LOSER" IS GEORGE BUSH, EVEN THOUGH HE "WON."
The Losers
Bush 58%
Buchanan 40%
Tsongas 35%
Clinton 26%
Kerrey 12%
Harkin 10%
Brown 9%
PAT BUCHANAN "LOST," BUT "WON" BECAUSE BUSH "LOST" SO MANY VOTES FROM PEOPLE WHO DON'T REALLY WANT BUCHANAN TO "WIN" THE WHITE HOUSE.
Buchanan 40%
TSONGAS "LOST" BY GETTING A SMALLER "WIN" THAN AT LEAST ONE POLL PREDICTED, BUT FOR SOMEONE WHO EVERYBODY EXPECTS TO "LOSE," HE DID "WIN."
Tsongas 35%
CLINTON "LOST" BECAUSE HE ONCE HAD BEEN EXPECTED TO "WIN," BUT "WON" BECAUSE IT LOOKED FOR A MINUTE LIKE HE'D "LOSE" MUCH WORSE.
Clinton 26%
THE OTHERS JUST "LOST."
Kerrey
Harkin
Brown
ANY QUESTIONS?
DOES THIS NARROW THE FIELD?

Hillary

Jeff Danziger

"I suppose I could have stayed home and baked cookies and had teas . . . ," Hillary Clinton, the governor's wife said, in a pique that created one of the major stirs of the campaign. Mrs. Clinton's remarks, made in response to questions about her law practice, were seen as a slap at homemakers. She later tried to salve the wound by offering a chocolate-chip cookie recipe of her own.

Danziger in *The Christian Science Monitor* ©1992 TCSPS

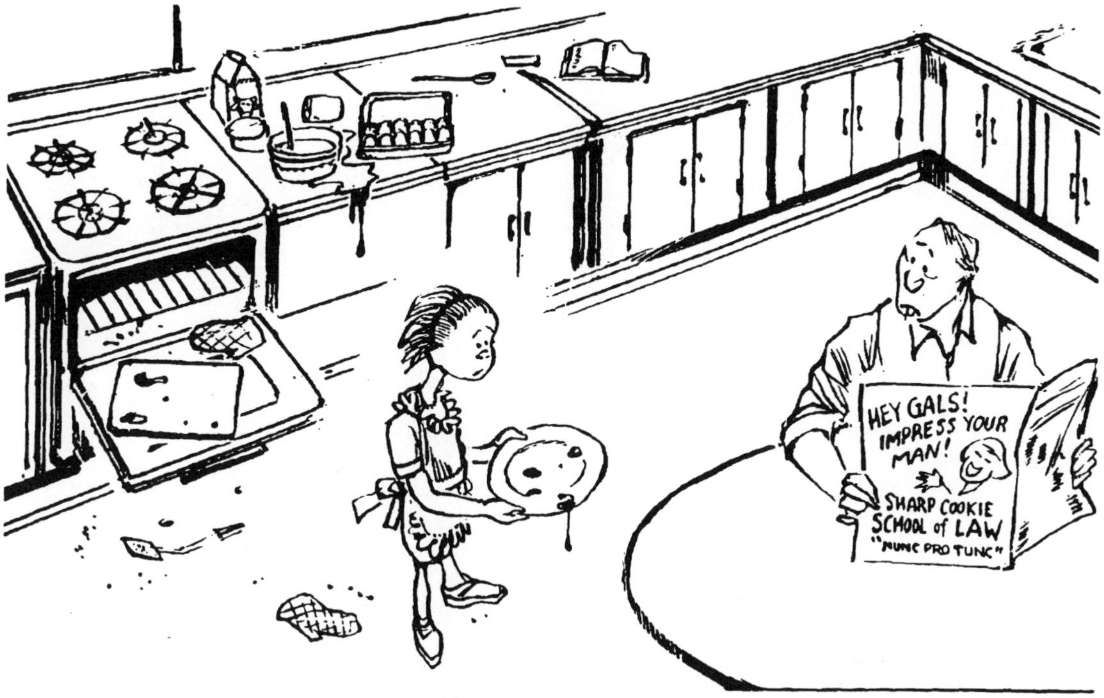
HEY GALS!
IMPRESS YOUR
MAN!
SHARP COOKIE
SCHOOL of LAW
"NUNC PRO TUNC"

GREAT MOMENTS in AMERICAN LAW
HILLARY CLINTON'S FIRST BATCH OF COOKIES

Bob Gorrell

Politics was an all-in-the-family affair, as both parties pitched their own brand of family values. The writings of Hillary Clinton, who once argued that children should have the legal right to separate from negligent parents, became a focal point of the family-values debate.

Bob Gorrell, *Richmond Times-Dispatch*

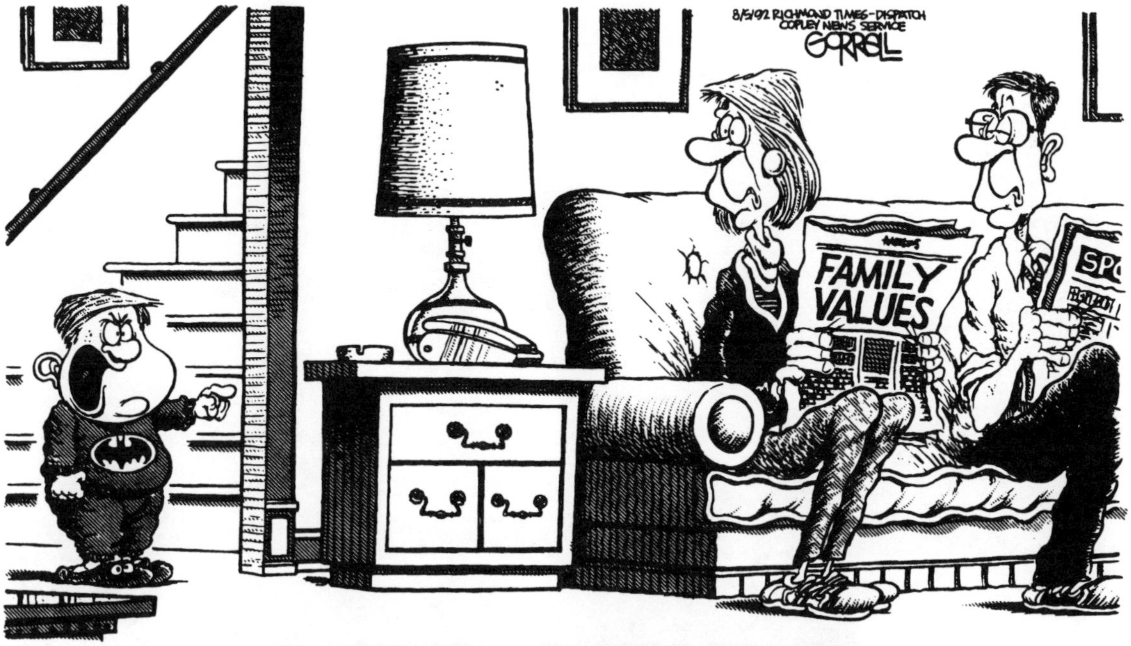
8/5/92 RICHMOND TIMES-DISPATCH
COPLEY NEWS SERVICE
GORRELL
FAMILY VALUES

**"HILLARY CLINTON SAYS I DON'T *HAVE* TO TAKE A BATH! . . .
HILLARY CLINTON SAYS I DON'T *HAVE* TO GO TO BED! . . .
HILLARY CLINTON SAYS MY LAWYER CAN DRAG *YOU* INTO *COURT!*"**

Rex Babin

Clinton said the public would be getting two for one if they voted for him.

Rex Babin, *Albany Times Union*

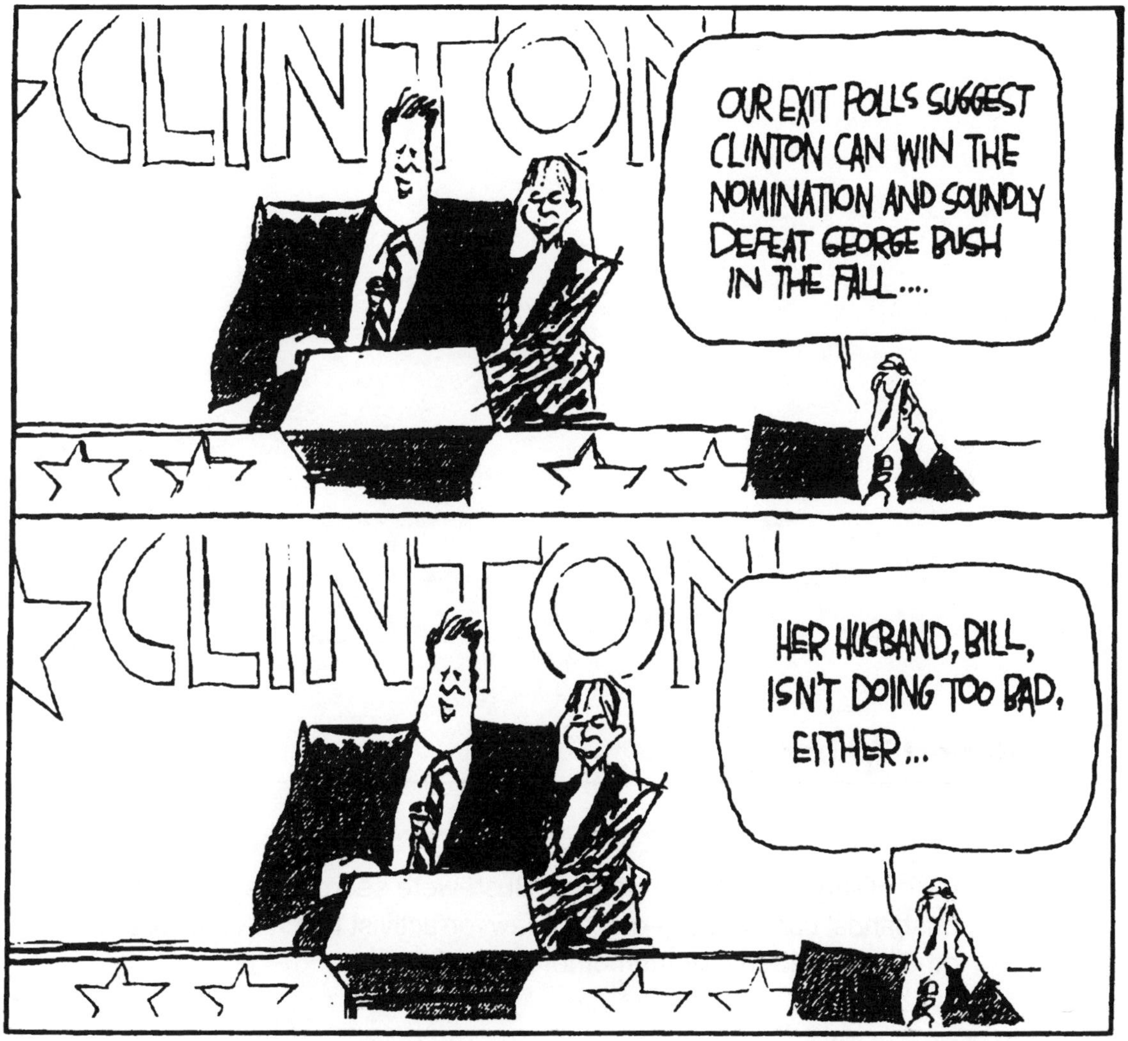
CLINTON
OUR EXIT POLLS SUGGEST CLINTON CAN WIN THE NOMINATION AND SOUNDLY DEFEAT GEORGE BUSH IN THE FALL....
CLINTON
HER HUSBAND, BILL, ISN'T DOING TOO BAD, EITHER...

Robert Weber

Both Hillary Clinton and Barbara Bush were seen as assets to their husbands' campaigns—one, the lawyer-activist in a headband; the other, the maternal grandmother in pearls.

"Betsy and I feel that this election comes down to
just one thing—who has the better wife."

The Bubba Factor

William Costello

Despite his Ivy-League polish, Clinton never disavowed his Dixie roots. In between his policy-wonk expressions, Clinton threw out homespun phrases. Soon, everyone was asking, "Just what is a lick log?"

For *USA Today*. Courtesy of William Costello and *USA Today*

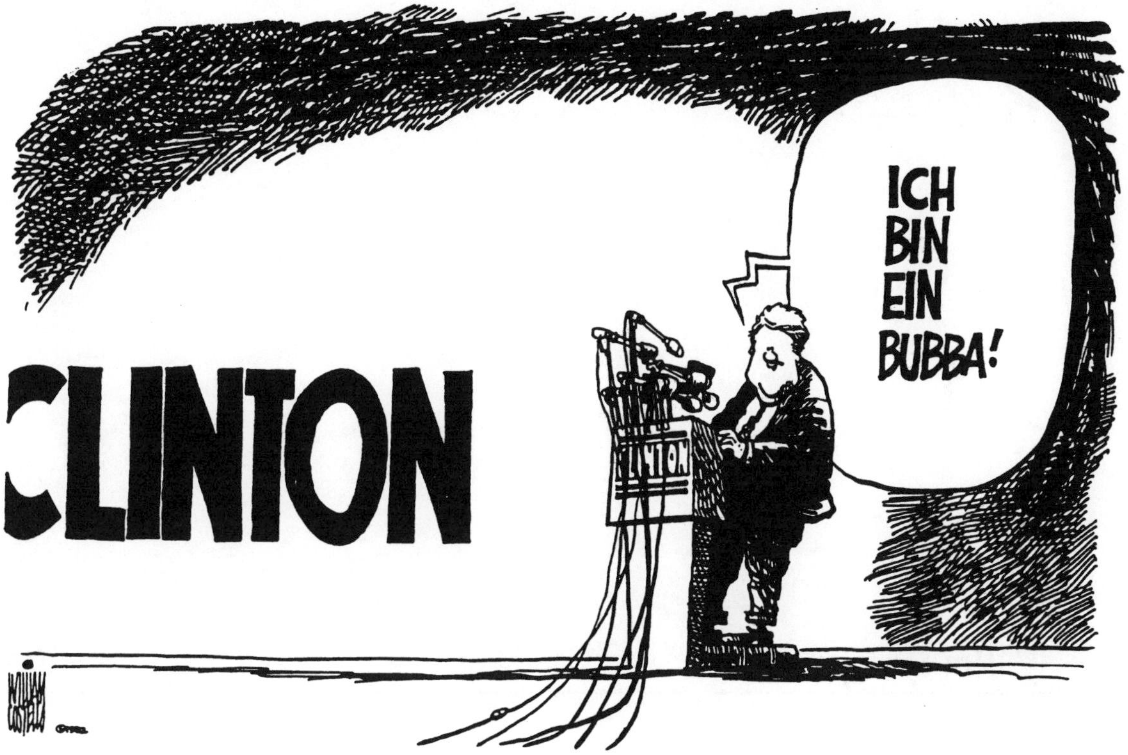
CLINTON
ICH BIN EIN BUBBA!

JFK

Jim Borgman

With hand in pocket, Clinton patterned himself after his political idol, John F. Kennedy. Clinton decided politics was for him at age sixteen, after shaking hands with Kennedy in a Rose Garden ceremony as a delegate to Boys Nation.

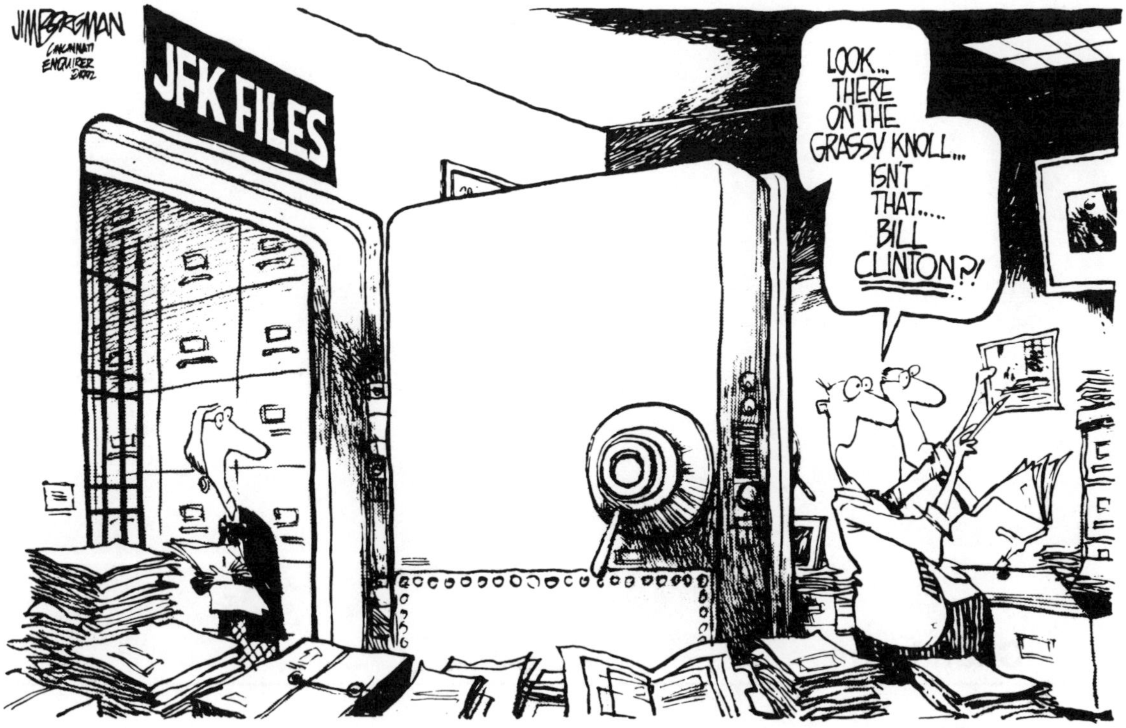
JIM BORGMAN
CINCINNATI ENQUIRER
JFK FILES
LOOK... THERE ON THE GRASSY KNOLL... ISN'T THAT..... BILL CLINTON?!

Inhale

Chan Lowe

And then there was pot. During a campaign debate in New York, Clinton was asked if he'd ever broken any drug laws. He admitted experimenting with marijuana during his days at Oxford but said he had not inhaled.

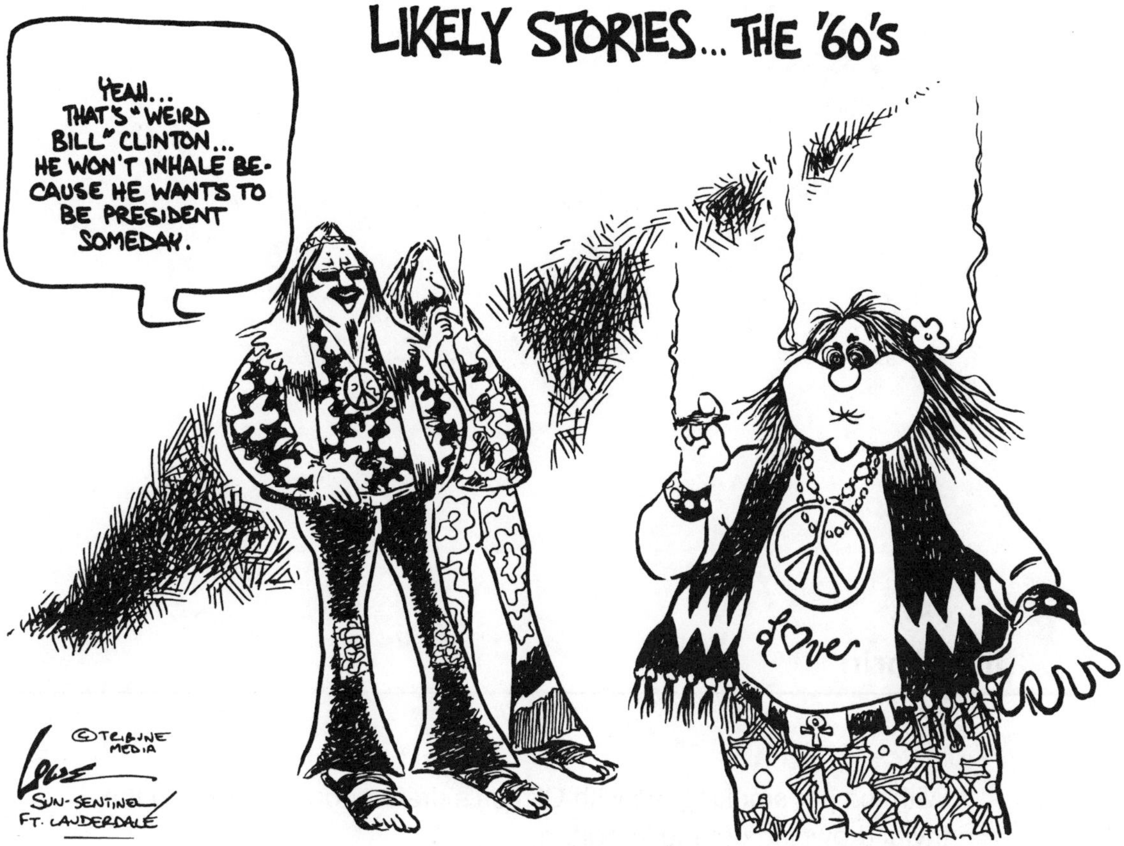
LIKELY STORIES... THE '60'S
YEAH... THAT'S "WEIRD BILL" CLINTON... HE WON'T INHALE BE-CAUSE HE WANTS TO BE PRESIDENT SOMEDAY.
Love
©TRIBUNE MEDIA
SUN-SENTINEL FT. LAUDERDALE

Jim Morin

With the pot smoking, as with Clinton's draft record, some saw the trivial drowning out the important.

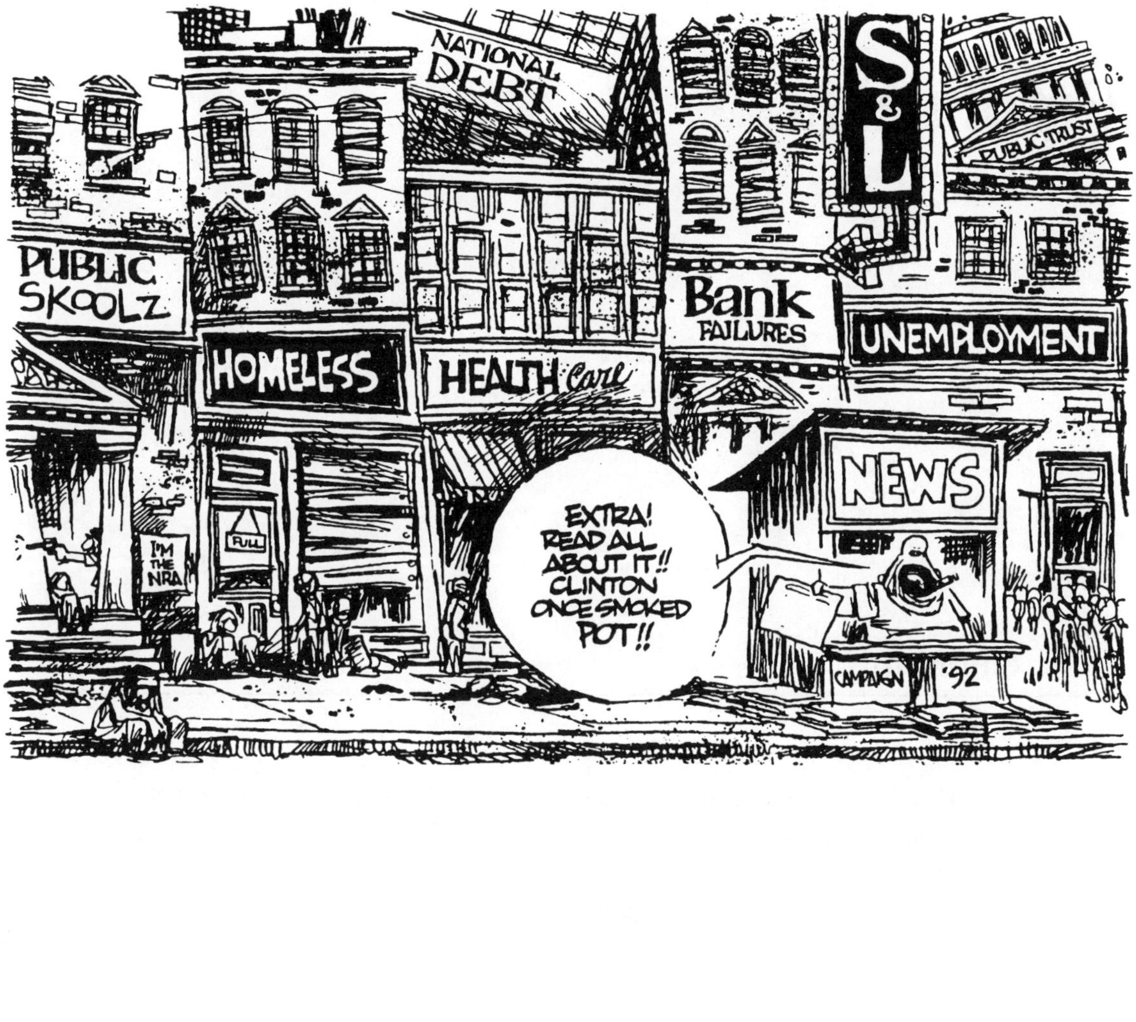
NATIONAL DEBT
S&L
PUBLIC TRUST
PUBLIC SKOOLZ
HOMELESS
HEALTH Care
Bank FAILURES
UNEMPLOYMENT
NEWS
I'M THE NRA
FULL
EXTRA! READ ALL ABOUT IT!! CLINTON ONCE SMOKED POT!!
CAMPAIGN '92

Perotmania

Oliphant

From talk-show madness came a third-party hurricane out of the blue called Ross Perot.

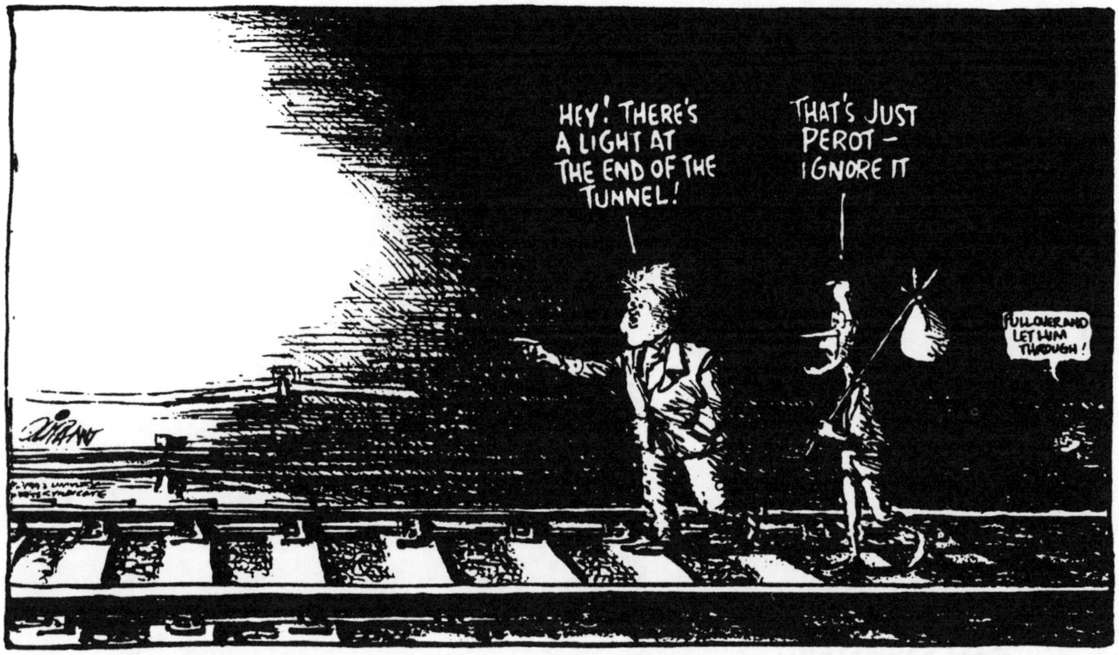
HEY! THERE'S A LIGHT AT THE END OF THE TUNNEL!
THAT'S JUST PEROT - IGNORE IT
PULL OVER AND LET HIM THROUGH!

Jeff MacNelly

Democrats and Republicans alike didn't know what to make of the diminutive Texas billionaire.

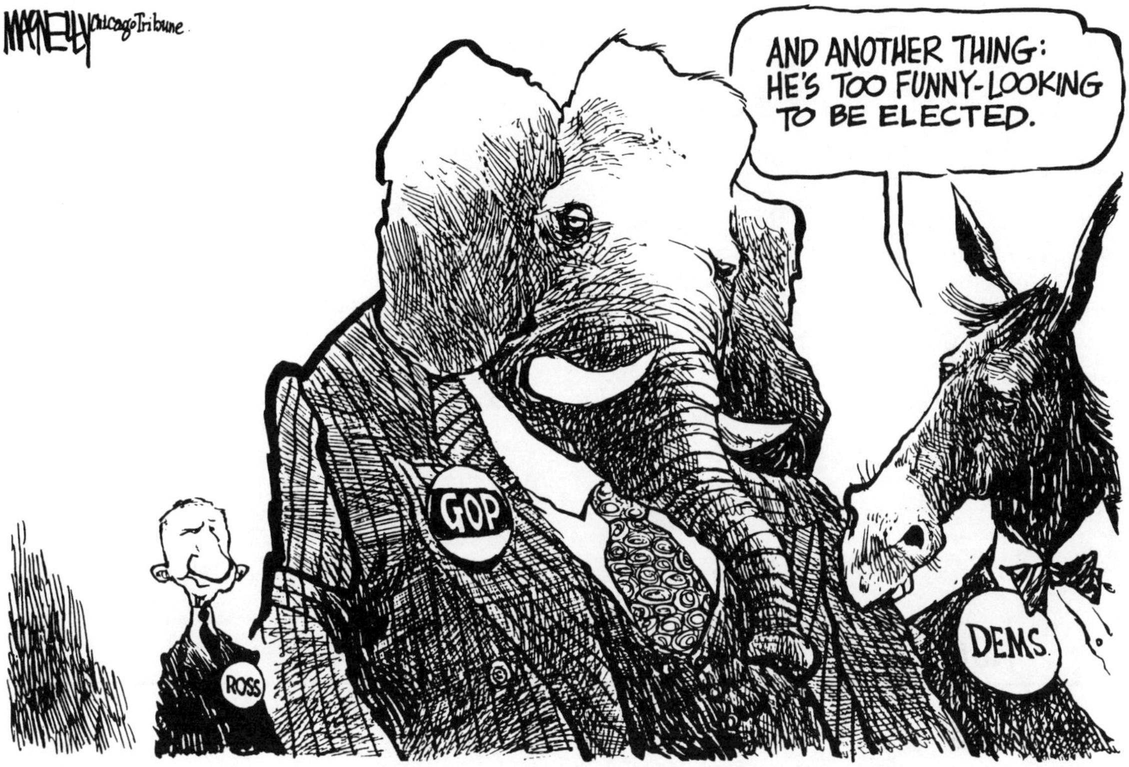
MACNELLY Chicago Tribune
AND ANOTHER THING: HE'S TOO FUNNY-LOOKING TO BE ELECTED.
GOP
ROSS
DEMS.

AUTH

Perot spoke a simple message compared with those of the other two candidates. Voters increasingly took to his plain-spokenness.

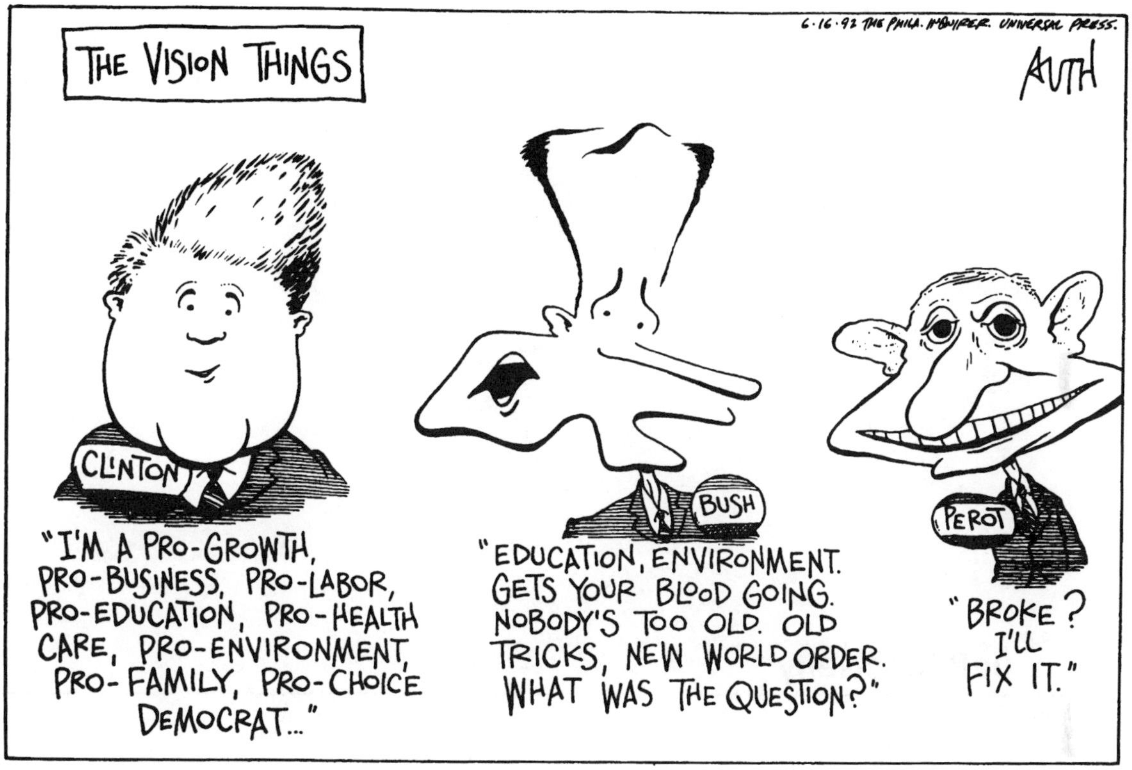
THE VISION THINGS
6·16·92 THE PHILA. INQUIRER. UNIVERSAL PRESS.
AUTH
CLINTON
BUSH
PEROT
"I'M A PRO-GROWTH, PRO-BUSINESS, PRO-LABOR, PRO-EDUCATION, PRO-HEALTH CARE, PRO-ENVIRONMENT, PRO-FAMILY, PRO-CHOICE DEMOCRAT..."
"EDUCATION, ENVIRONMENT. GETS YOUR BLOOD GOING. NOBODY'S TOO OLD. OLD TRICKS, NEW WORLD ORDER. WHAT WAS THE QUESTION?"
"BROKE? I'LL FIX IT."

Jeff MacNelly

Perot's candidacy caught fire, and the two major parties started to get nervous.

Reprinted by permission: Tribune Media Services

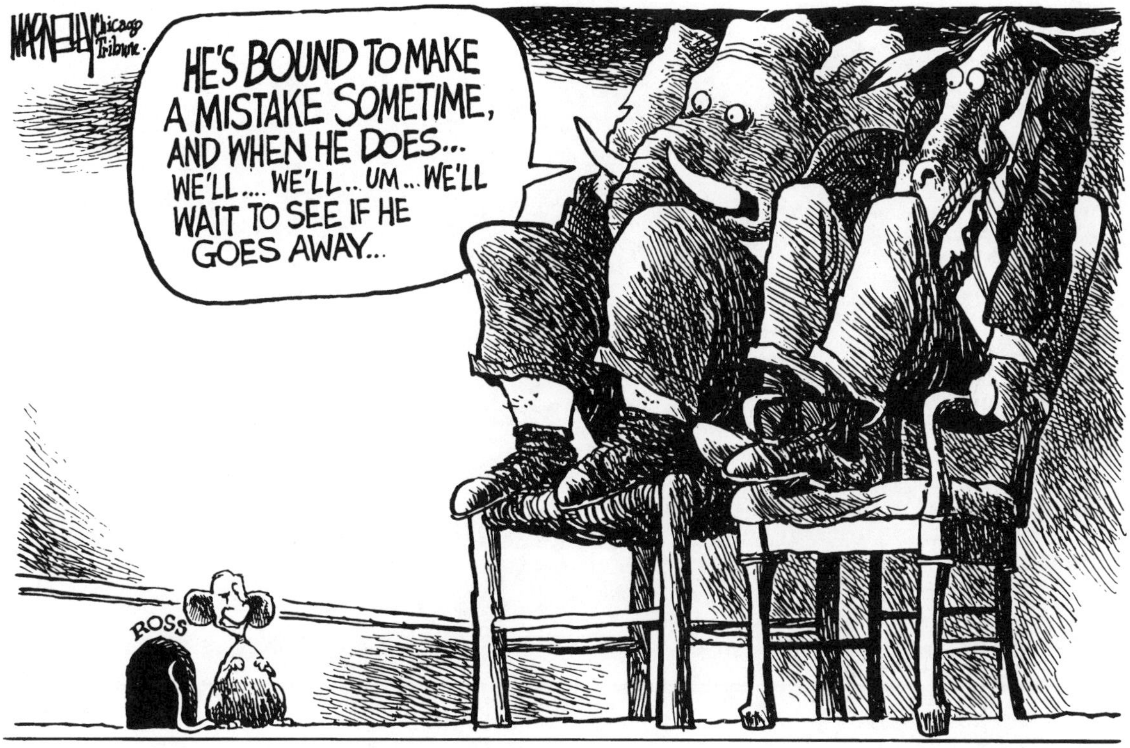
MACNELLY Chicago Tribune
HE'S BOUND TO MAKE A MISTAKE SOMETIME, AND WHEN HE DOES... WE'LL.... WE'LL... UM... WE'LL WAIT TO SEE IF HE GOES AWAY...
ROSS

Doug Marlette

When spring turned to summer, Clinton was running third in the polls behind Perot and Bush and was struggling to regain momentum.

Creators Syndicate

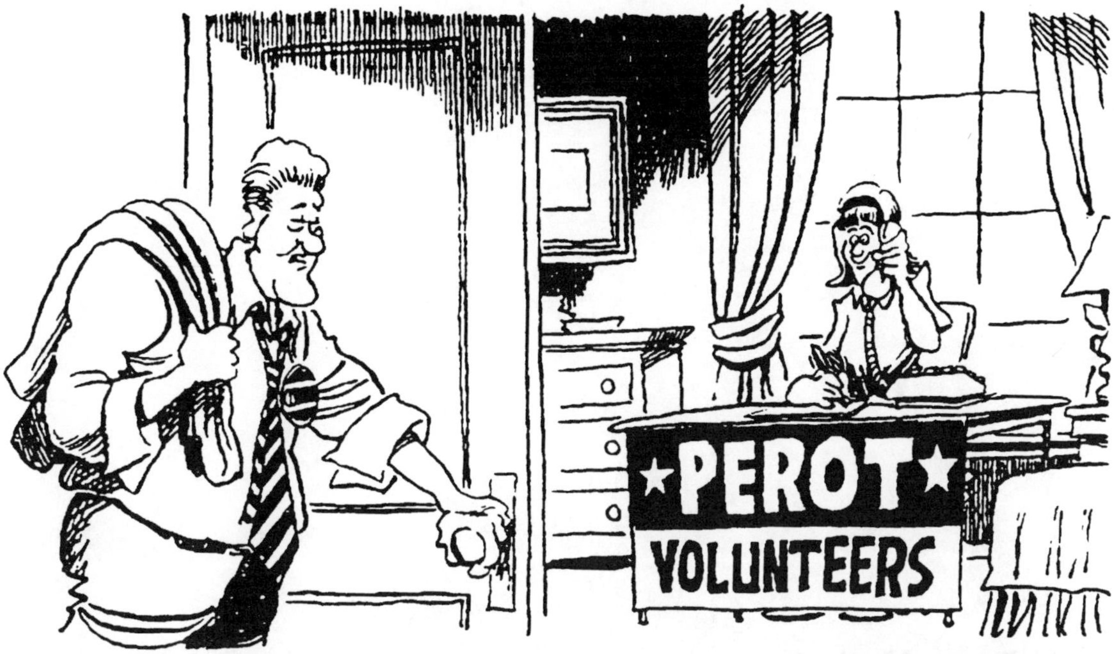
★PEROT★
VOLUNTEERS

BY MARLETTE FOR NEW YORK NEWSDAY

"WE'RE LAGGING IN THE POLLS, THE CAMPAIGN'S STALLED, BROWN WON'T GO AWAY, THE MEDIA IGNORE US!... OH, WELL, AT LEAST THINGS CAN'T GET ANY WORSE, RIGHT, HILLARY?!..."

Doug Marlette

Clinton came to be regarded as the odd man out, with Perot and Bush in the center ring.

Creators Syndicate

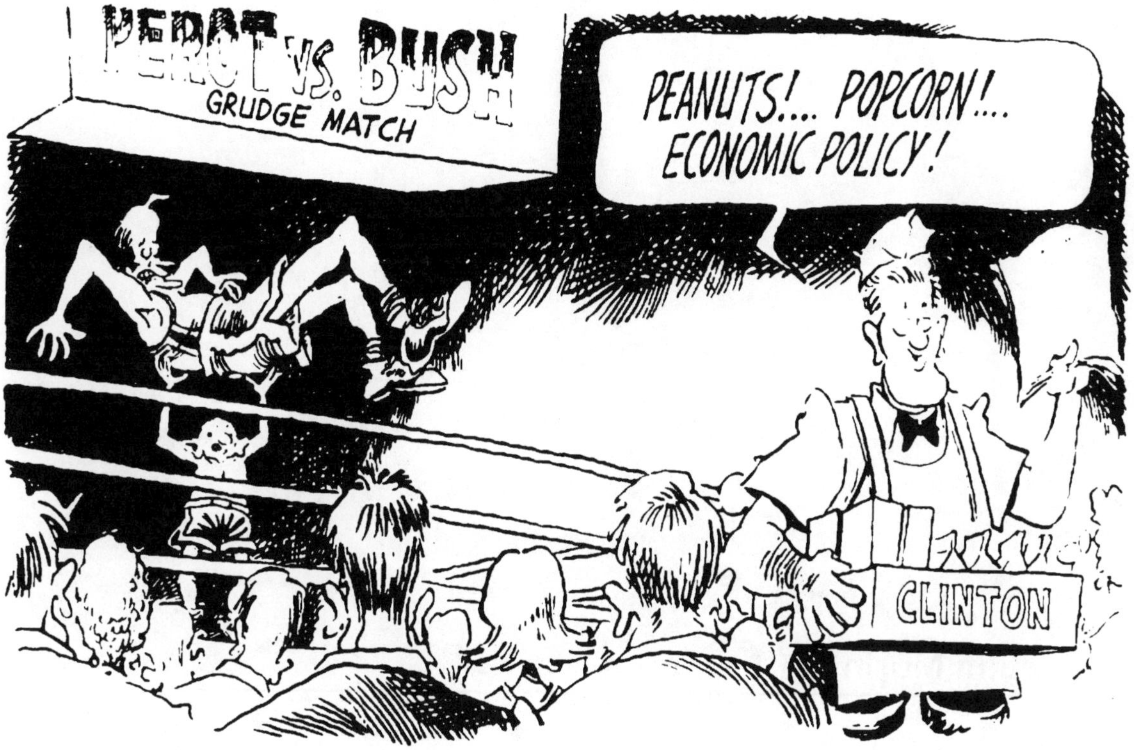
PEROT vs. BUSH
GRUDGE MATCH
PEANUTS!... POPCORN!... ECONOMIC POLICY!
CLINTON

Jim Morin

While Clinton tried to talk issues, the press focus was somewhere else.

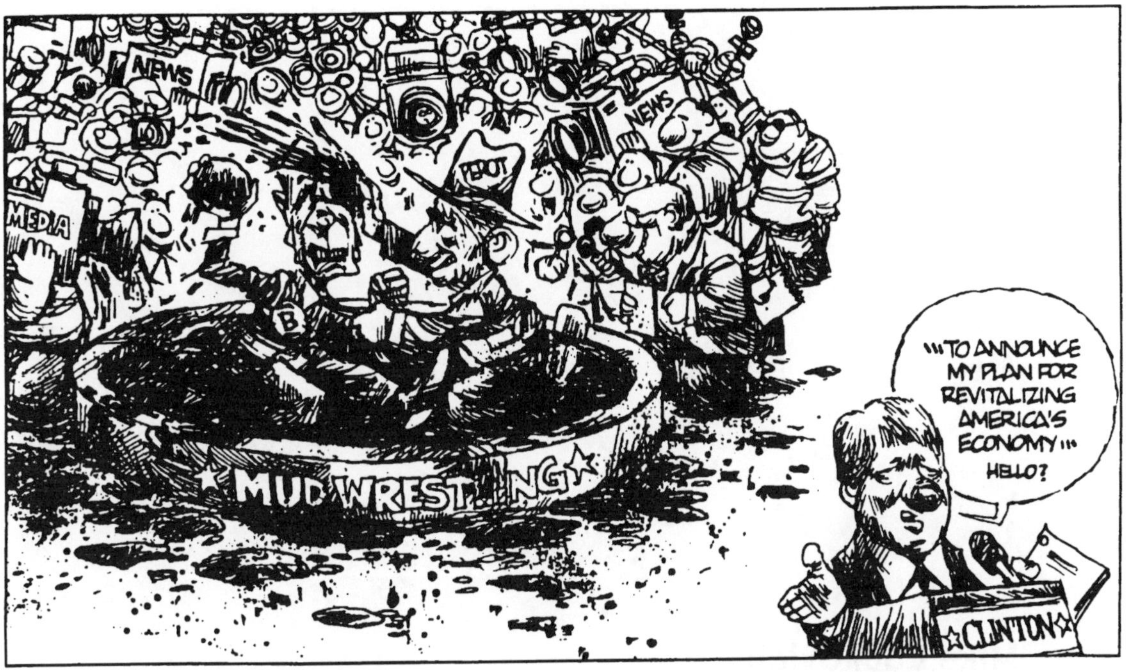
NEWS
NEWS
PEROT
MEDIA
B
★MUD WRESTL...NG★
...TO ANNOUNCE MY PLAN FOR REVITALIZING AMERICA'S ECONOMY...
HELLO?
☆CLINTON☆

Mike Luckovich

With three candidates in the race, polls showed that voters were still more interested in a "none of the above" candidate.

Creators Syndicate

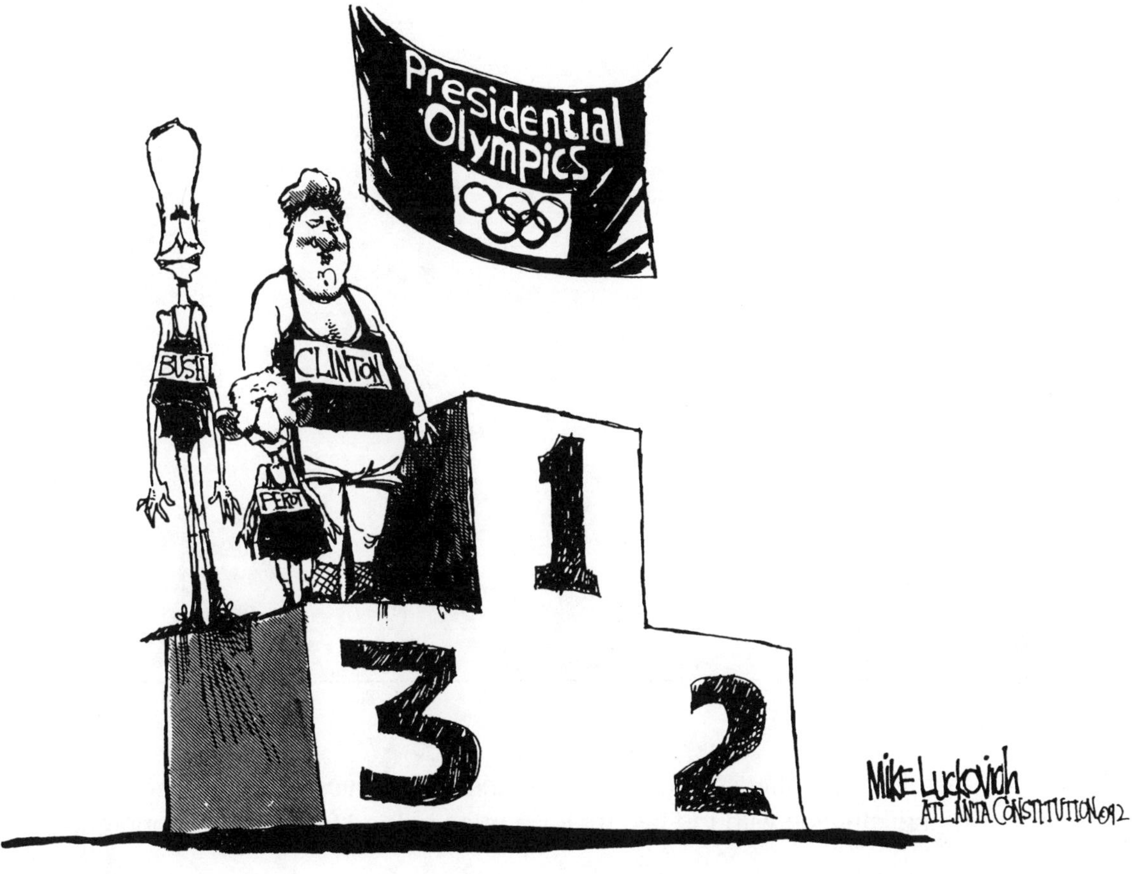
Presidential Olympics
BUSH
CLINTON
PEROT
1
3
2
MIKE Luckovich
ATLANTA CONSTITUTION ©92

AUTH

Perot's popularity sounded a death knell for politics as usual.
Dissatisfaction with the two major parties helped fuel Perot's popularity.

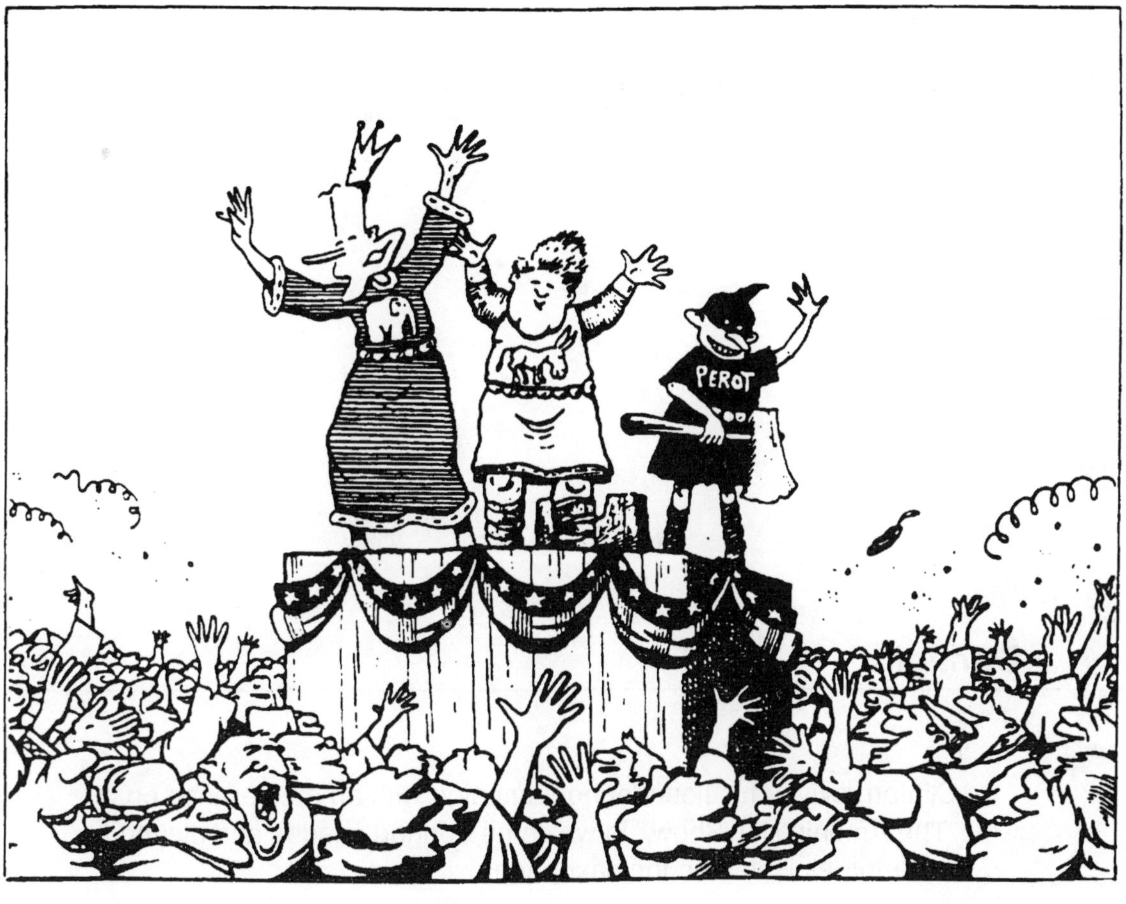
PEROT

Once More into the Breach

Dunagin

Clinton revived his floundering campaign with an appearance on "The Arsenio Hall Show," in which he donned shades and played "Heartbreak Hotel" on the saxophone.

Courtesy of *The Orlando Sentinel* and North America Syndicate, Inc.

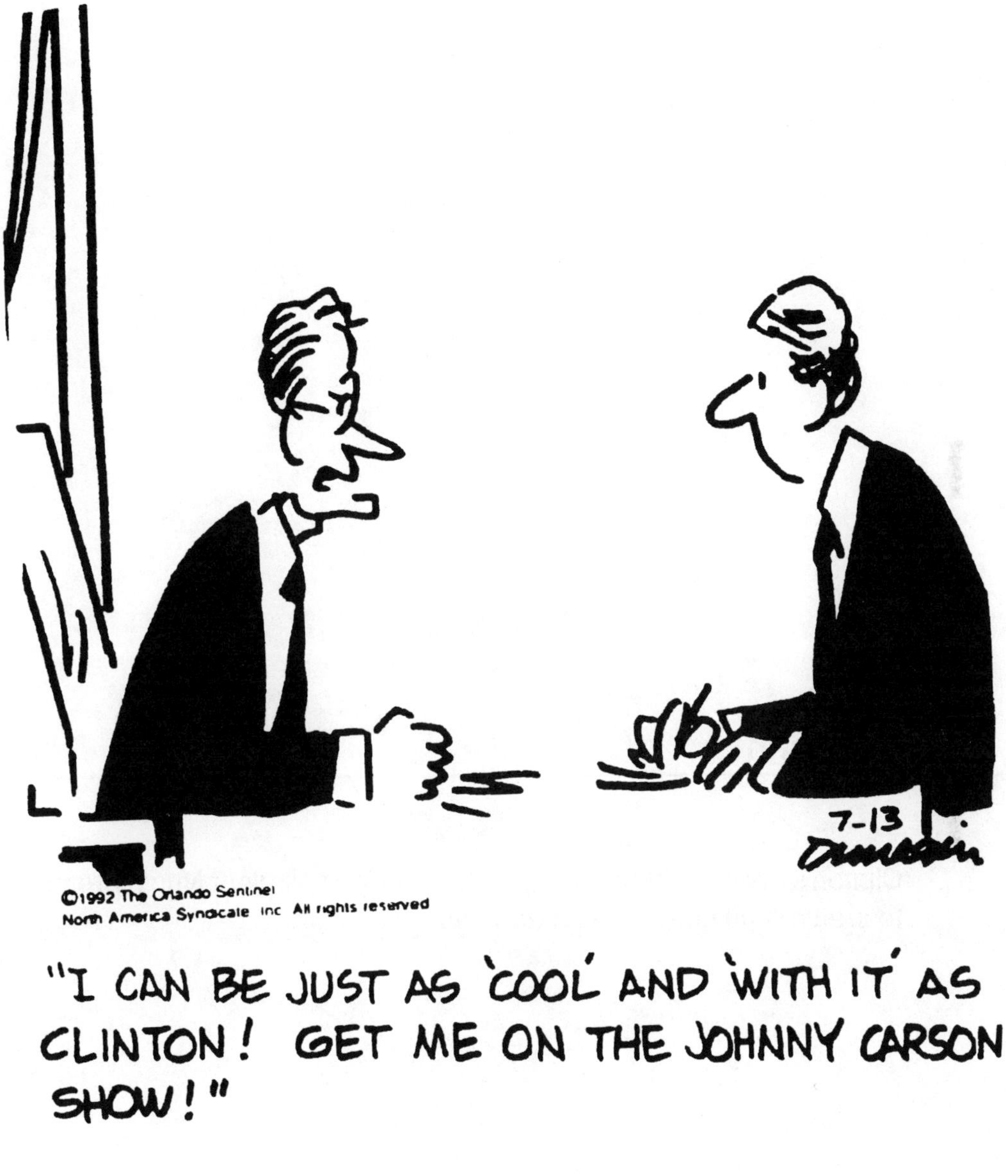
7-13
©1992 The Orlando Sentinel
North America Syndicate Inc All rights reserved

"I CAN BE JUST AS 'COOL' AND 'WITH IT' AS CLINTON! GET ME ON THE JOHNNY CARSON SHOW!"

Jack Ohman

Clinton's criticism of rap artist Sister Souljah's virulent lyrics threatened to create a rift between him and Jesse Jackson.

The Oregonian. Tribune Media Services

OLIPHANT
INTRODUCING THE HOT NEW RAPPER...
VICE-P
DON'T BE DISSIN' SISTER..
I WANNA BE VEEP MISTER...
GROVEL LIKE MIKE IN '88...
OR PEROT WILL BE MY RUNNING MATE...
JESSE FOR VP

Jack Ohman

While Clinton's choice of Sen. Al Gore was seen as politically smart, some wondered if the Tennessee Democrat might outshine the top of the ticket. Gore had run for president in 1988.

The Oregonian. Tribune Media Services

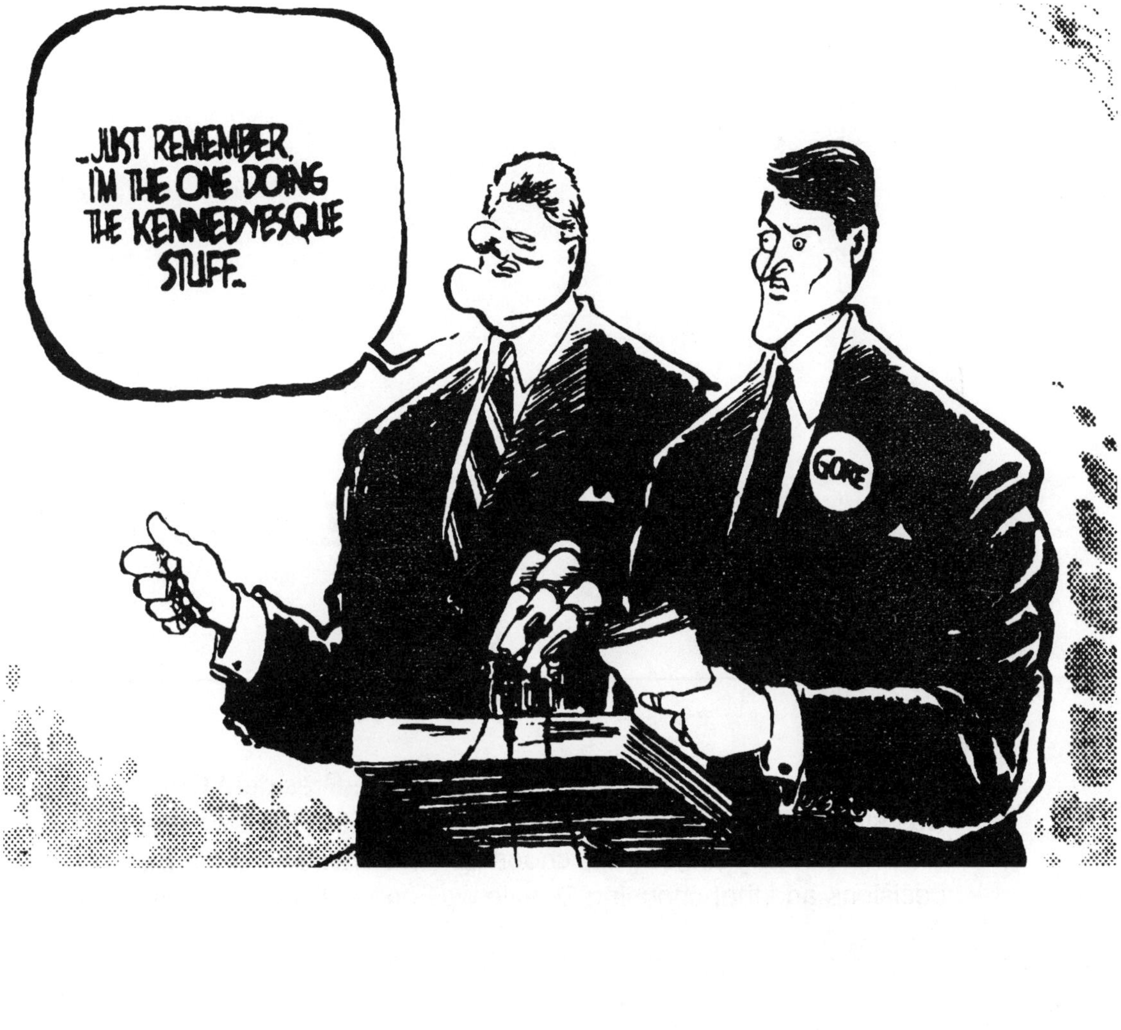
..JUST REMEMBER, I'M THE ONE DOING THE KENNEDYESQUE STUFF..
GORE

Oliphant

Gore was seen as more than a match for Vice-President Quayle, who was still having to live down his misspelling of the word potato(e). Clinton liked to point out that choosing Gore was one of his first decisions and that choosing Quayle was one of Bush's first decisions.

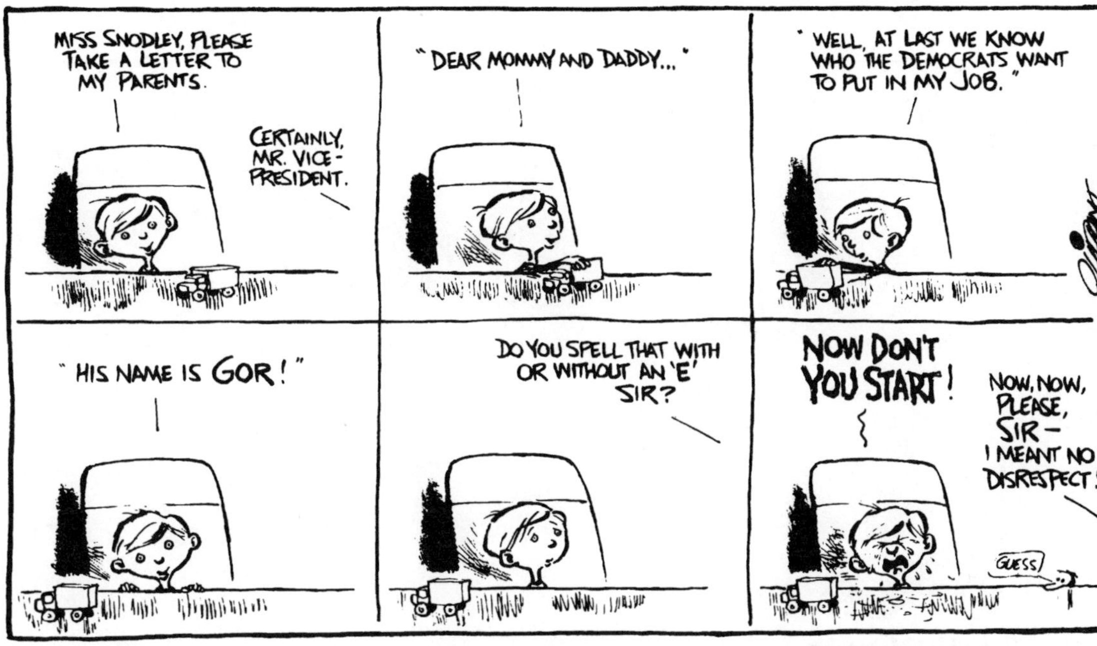
MISS SNODLEY, PLEASE TAKE A LETTER TO MY PARENTS.
CERTAINLY, MR. VICE-PRESIDENT.
"DEAR MOMMY AND DADDY..."
"WELL, AT LAST WE KNOW WHO THE DEMOCRATS WANT TO PUT IN MY JOB."
"HIS NAME IS GOR!"
DO YOU SPELL THAT WITH OR WITHOUT AN 'E' SIR?
NOW DON'T YOU START!
NOW, NOW, PLEASE, SIR – I MEANT NO DISRESPECT!
GUESS

Jack Ohman

Although he never posed a serious threat for the Democratic nomination, Jerry Brown, with the rhetorical style of an attack dog, pestered Clinton throughout the later primaries and into the convention.

The Oregonian. Tribune Media Services

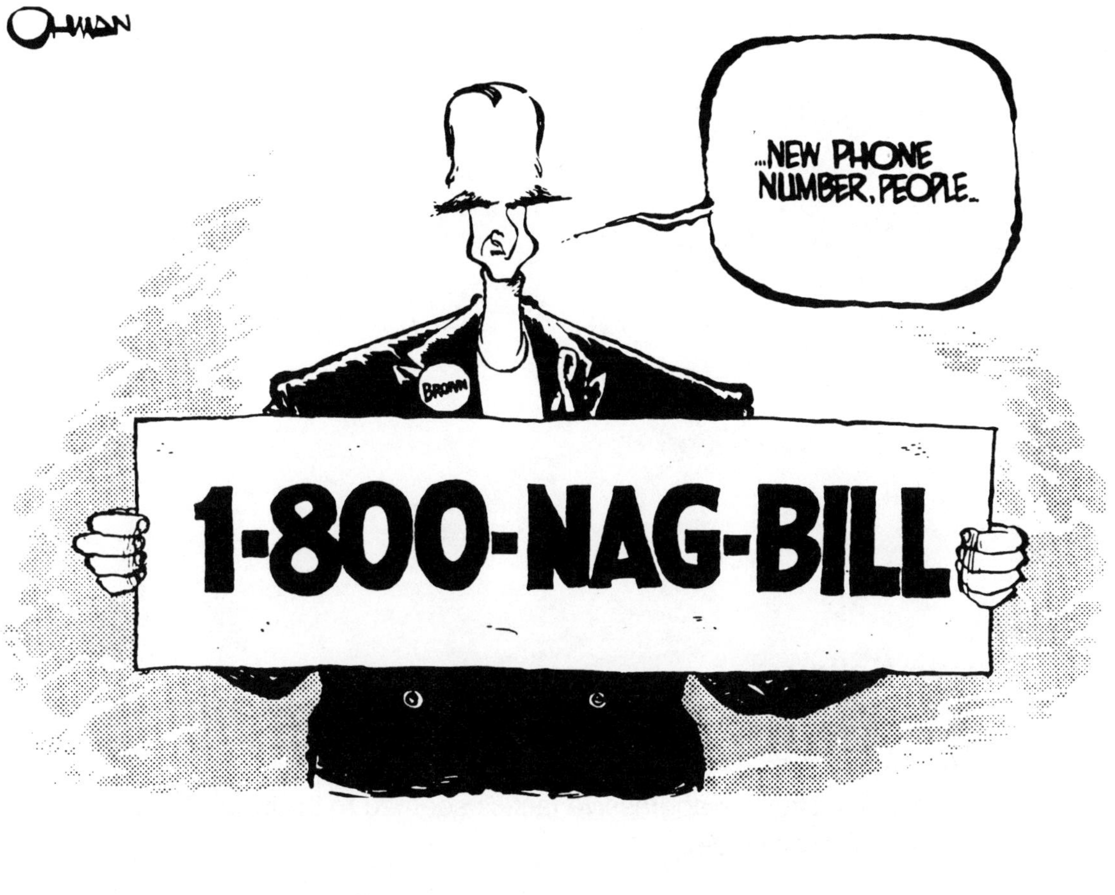
OHMAN
...NEW PHONE NUMBER, PEOPLE...
BROWN
1-800-NAG-BILL

Steve Kelley

At times, Brown's aggressive tactics seemed to throw the Clinton campaign off stride.

Copley News Service

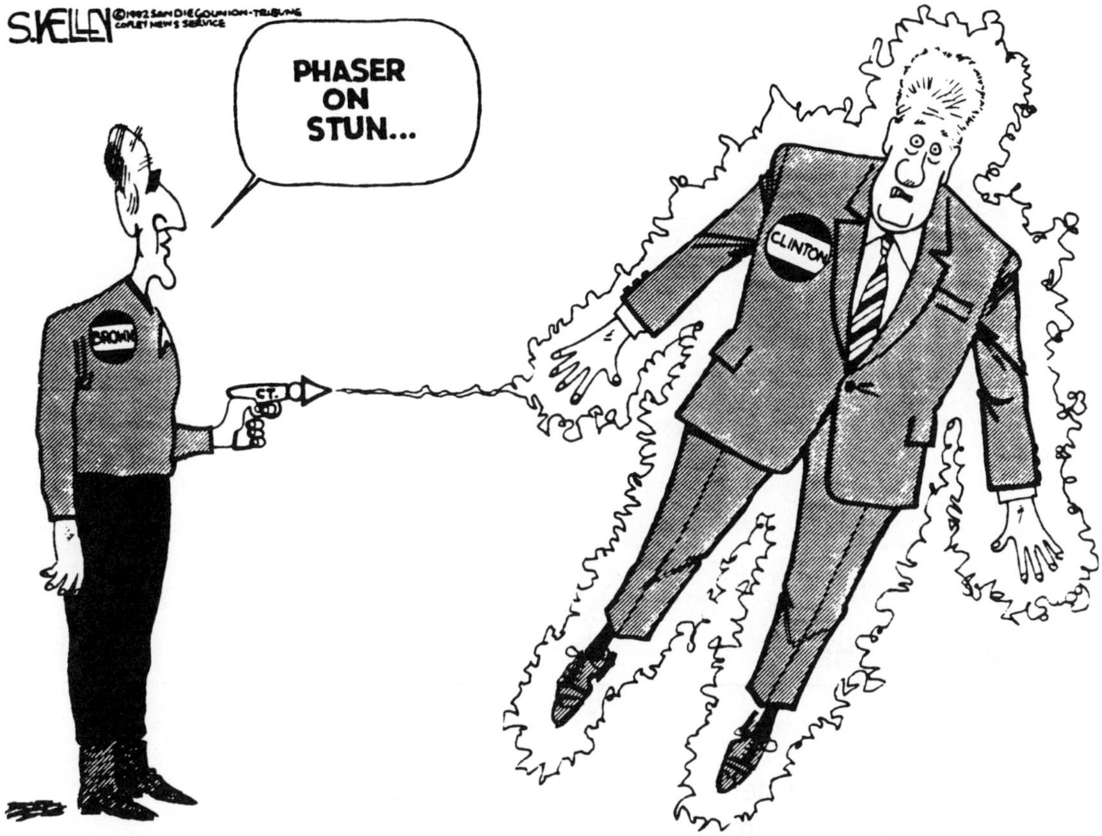
S.KELLEY ©1992 SAN DIEGO UNION-TRIBUNE COPLEY NEWS SERVICE
PHASER ON STUN...
BROWN
C.T.
CLINTON

Jack Ohman

Like the monster who wouldn't die, Clinton, the consummate campaigner, forged on to the nomination.

The Oregonian. Tribune Media Services

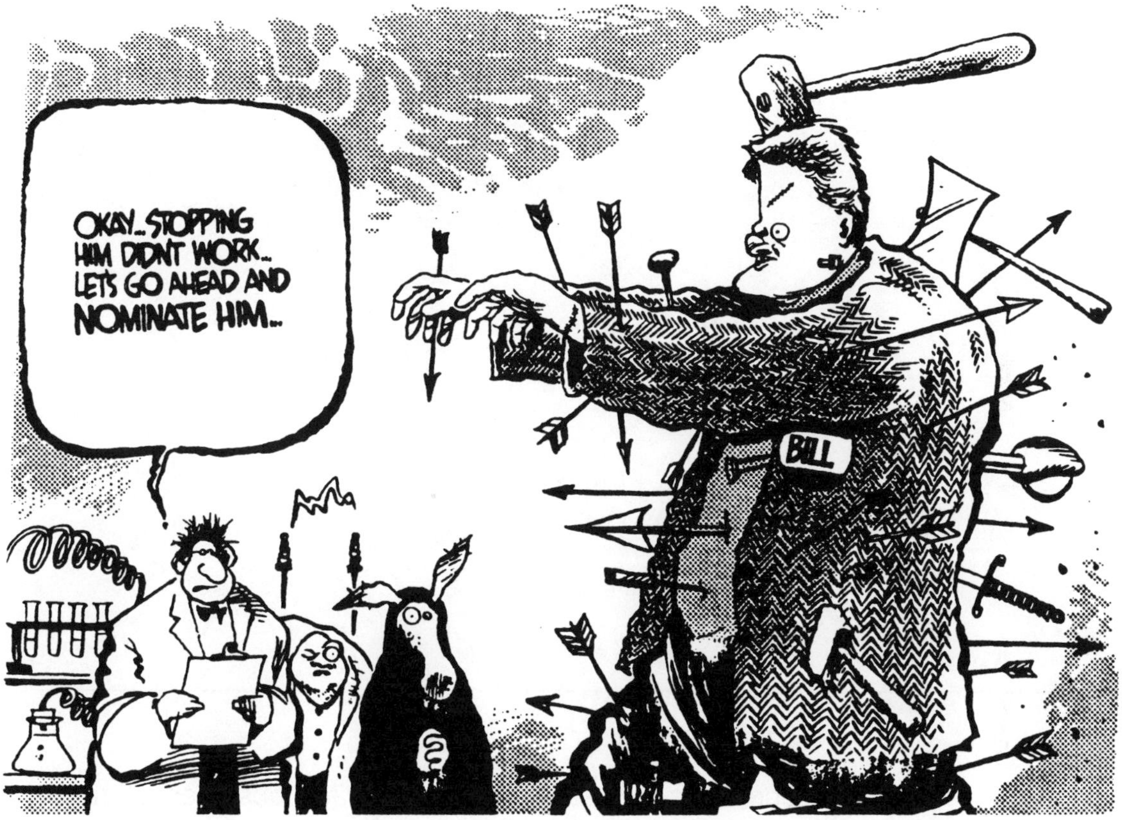
OKAY...STOPPING HIM DIDN'T WORK... LET'S GO AHEAD AND NOMINATE HIM...
BILL

AUTH

With the prospect of a Bush-Clinton race in the fall, observers started to weigh the baggage that both would bring to the race.

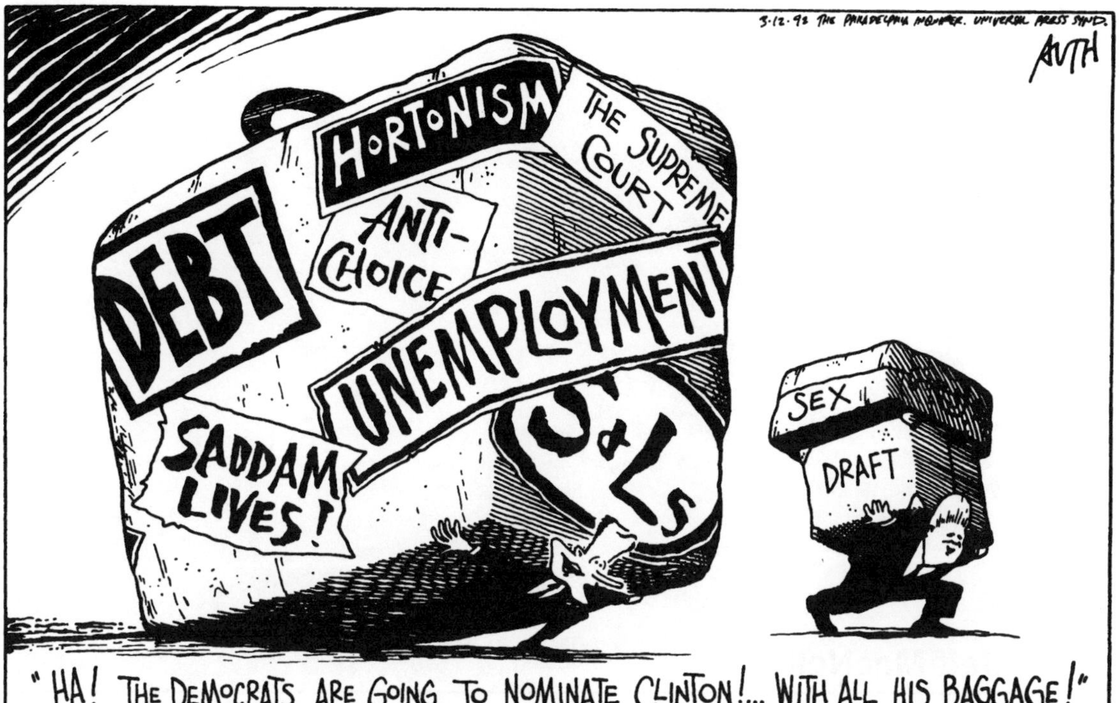
AUTH
HORTONISM
THE SUPREME COURT
DEBT
ANTI-CHOICE
UNEMPLOYMENT
SADDAM LIVES!
S&Ls
SEX
DRAFT

"HA! THE DEMOCRATS ARE GOING TO NOMINATE CLINTON!... WITH ALL HIS BAGGAGE!"

Jeff MacNelly

For Clinton, summer's big show was the Democratic National Convention in New York. Two moderate southerners, Clinton and Gore, were traveling to the land of New York, home to Gov. Mario Cuomo, an old-style liberal Democrat.

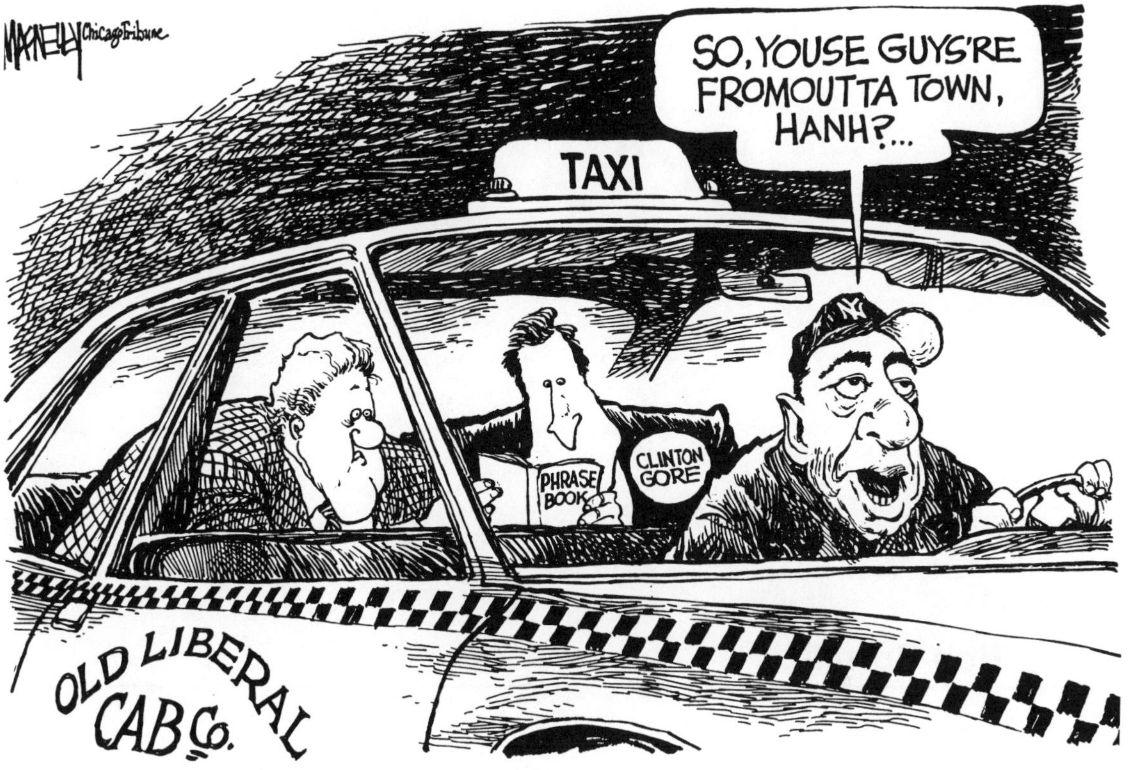
MACNELLY Chicago Tribune
SO, YOUSE GUYS'RE FROMOUTTA TOWN, HANH?...
TAXI
PHRASE BOOK
CLINTON GORE
OLD LIBERAL CAB CO.

Bob Gorrell

Even up until the convention, doubts remained among some
Democratic party faithful about Clinton's suitability to be the nominee.

Bob Gorrell, *Richmond Times-Dispatch*

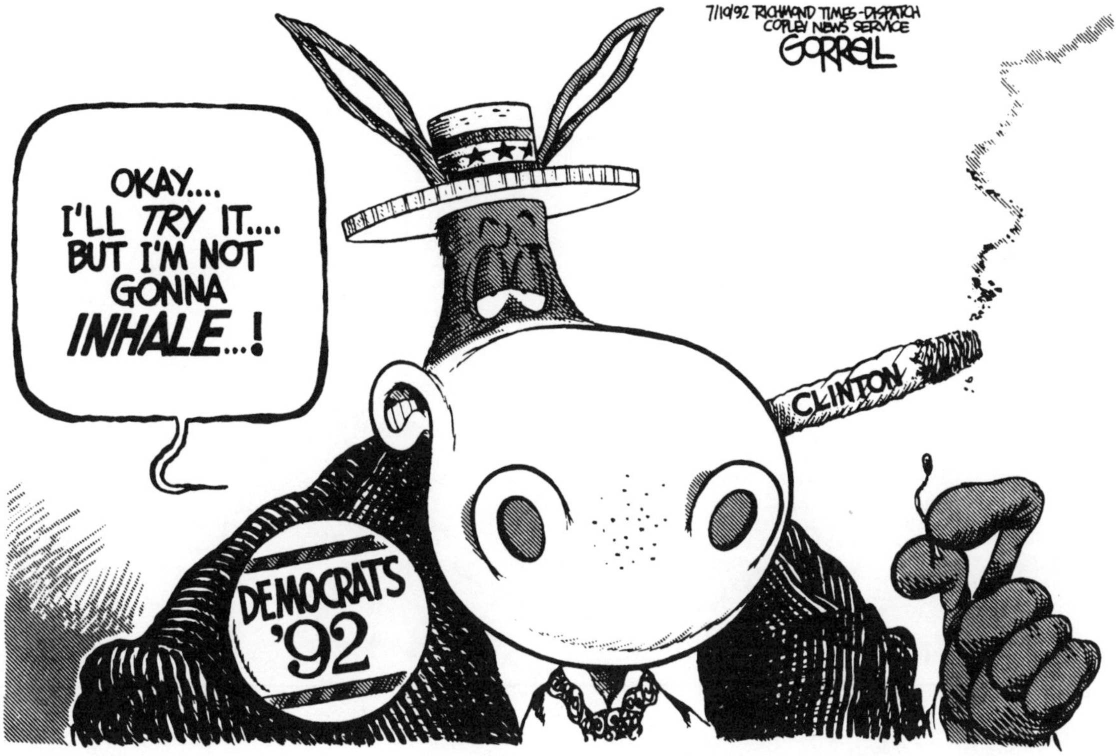
7/10/92 RICHMOND TIMES-DISPATCH
COPLEY NEWS SERVICE
GORRELL
OKAY.... I'LL TRY IT.... BUT I'M NOT GONNA INHALE...!
CLINTON
DEMOCRATS '92

Bob McGrath

With the nomination fight long concluded, the convention served as a coronation for Clinton, as the Perot and Bush camps looked on.

Bob McGrath for *American Caucus*

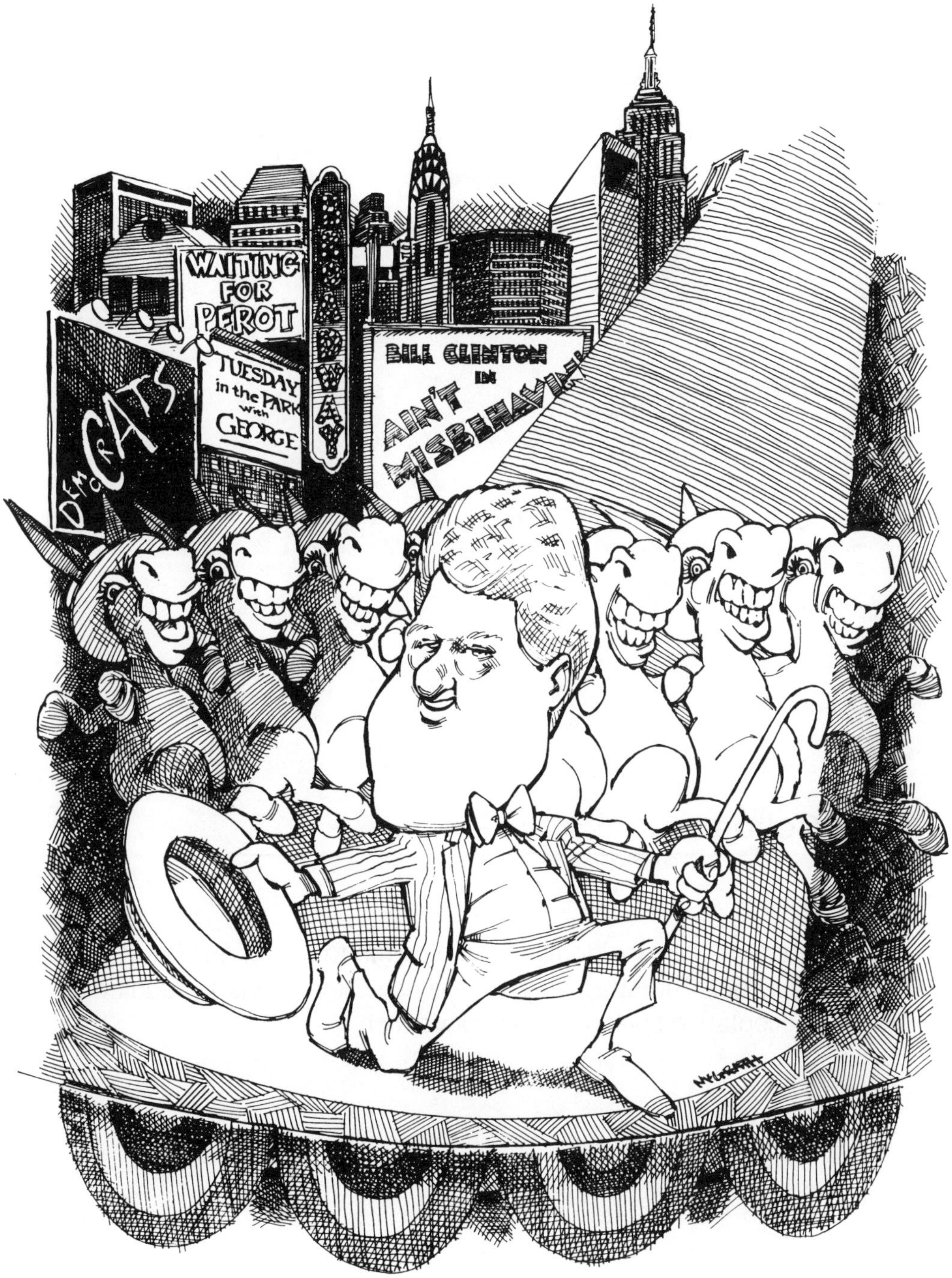

WAITING FOR PEROT
BROADWAY
DEMOCRATS
TUESDAY in the PARK with GEORGE
BILL CLINTON IN
AIN'T MISBEHAVIN'

Perot's Out

Mark Bolton

The heat of the presidential race became too much for Perot, who abruptly quit Thursday, July 16, the day Clinton was scheduled to give his acceptance speech at the convention.

Courtesy of Mark Bolton and *The* (Jackson) *Clarion-Ledger*

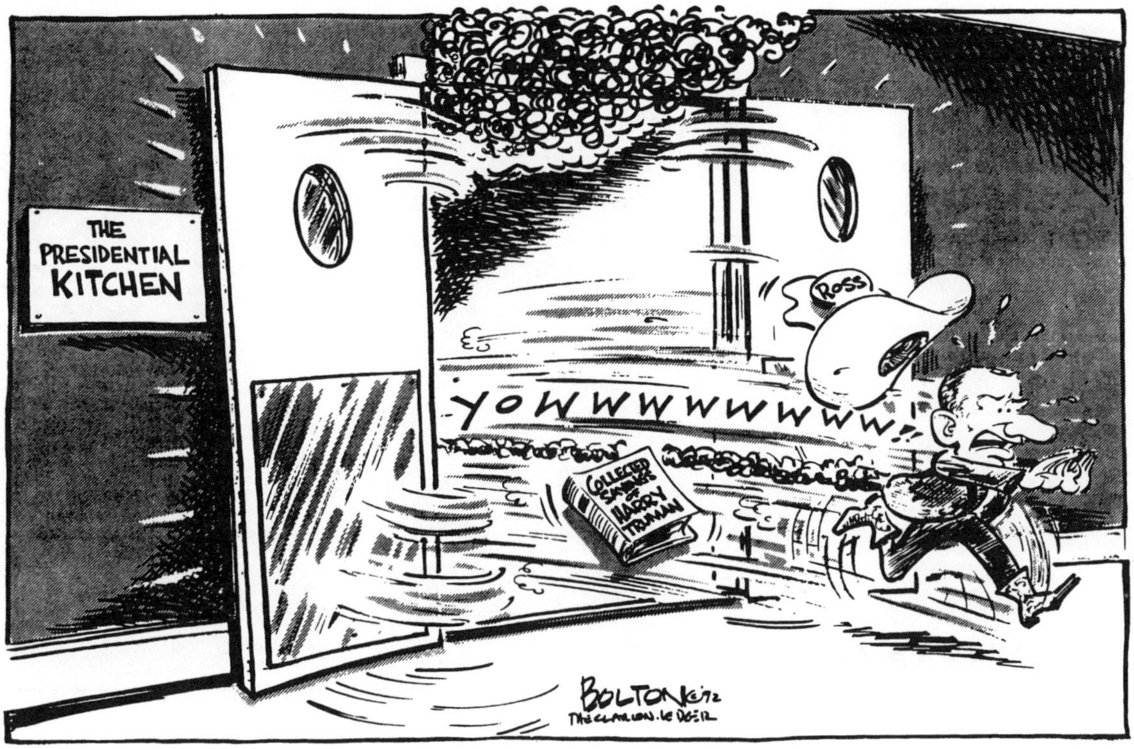
THE PRESIDENTIAL KITCHEN
ROSS
YOWWWWWWWWW!!
COLLECTED SAYINGS OF HARRY TRUMAN
BOLTON

Mike Keefe

While the Clinton and Bush campaigns looked toward the fall, Perot's withdrawal left his supporters without a candidate.

Mike Keefe, *The Denver Post*

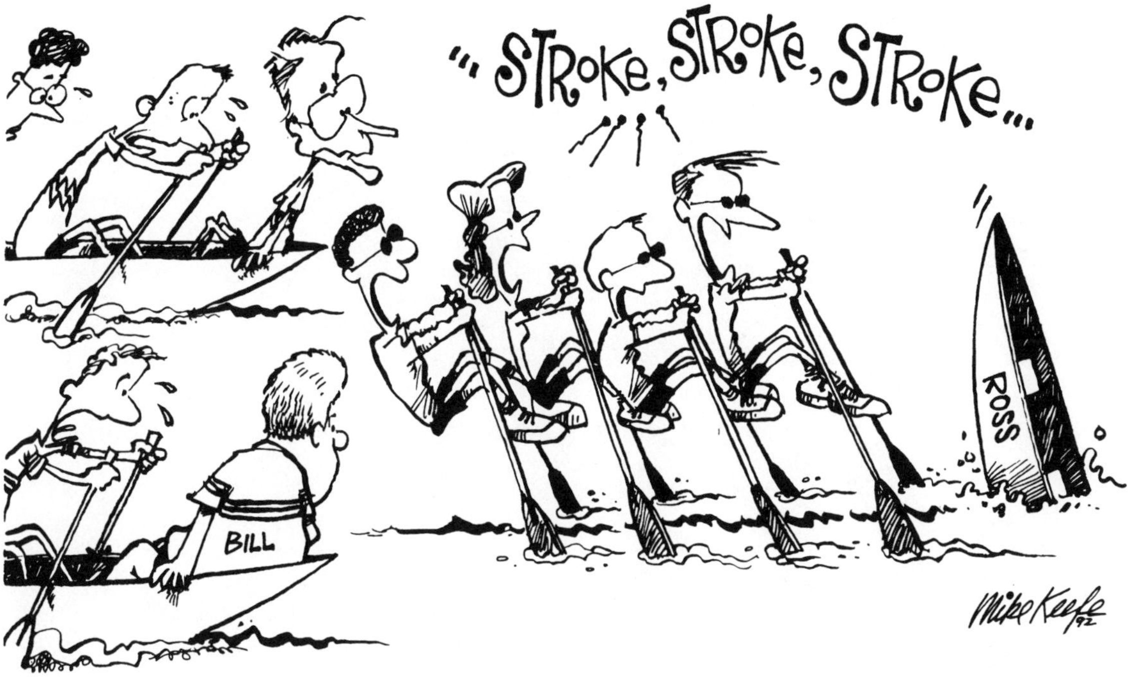
"... STROKE, STROKE, STROKE..."
BILL
ROSS
Mike Keefe '92

KAL

Both Clinton and Bush were anxious to sweep Perot supporters into their camps.

Cartoonists and Writers Syndicate

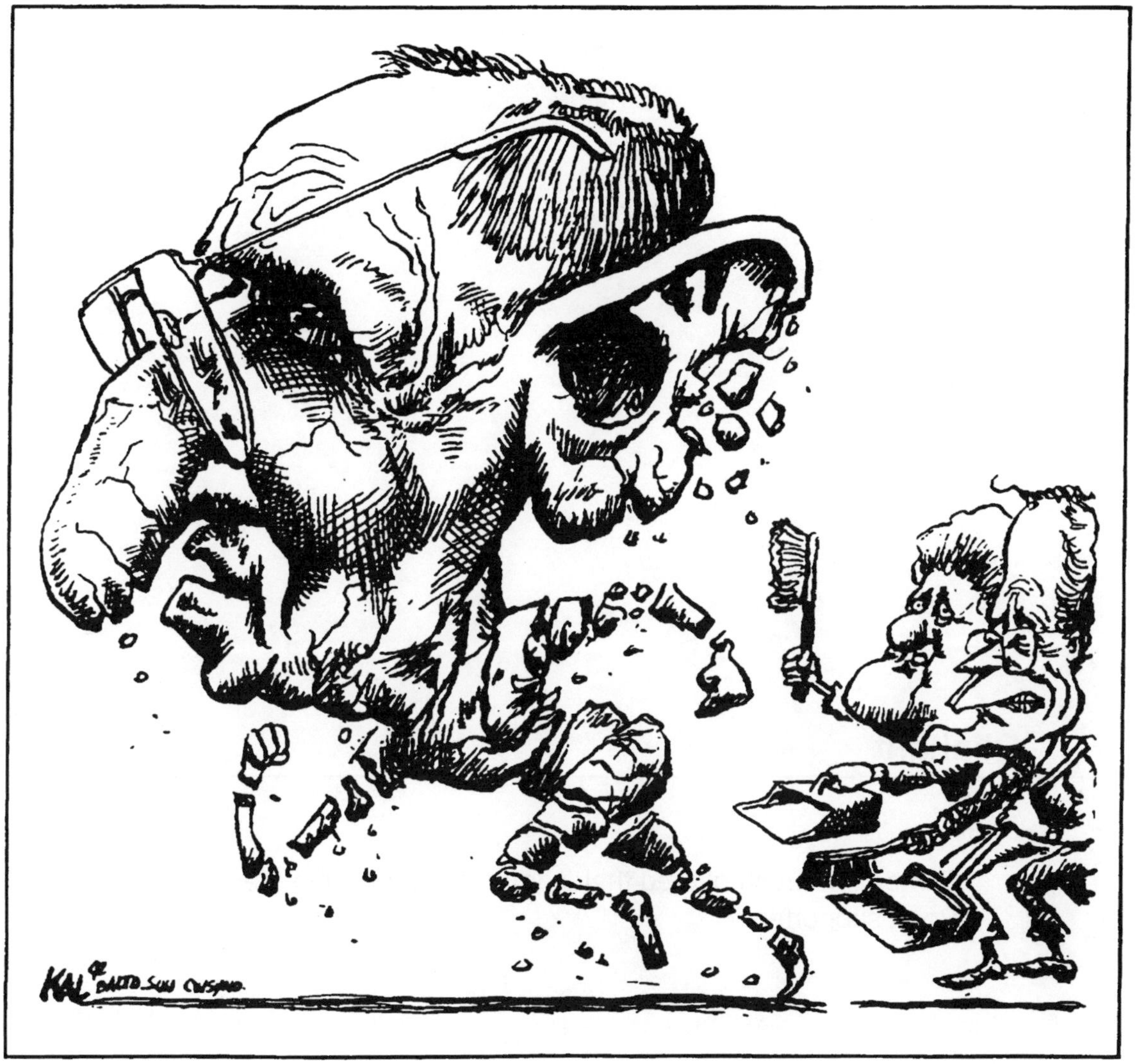
KAL

Oliphant

Clinton and Bush offered their campaigns as sanctuaries for grieving Perot supporters.

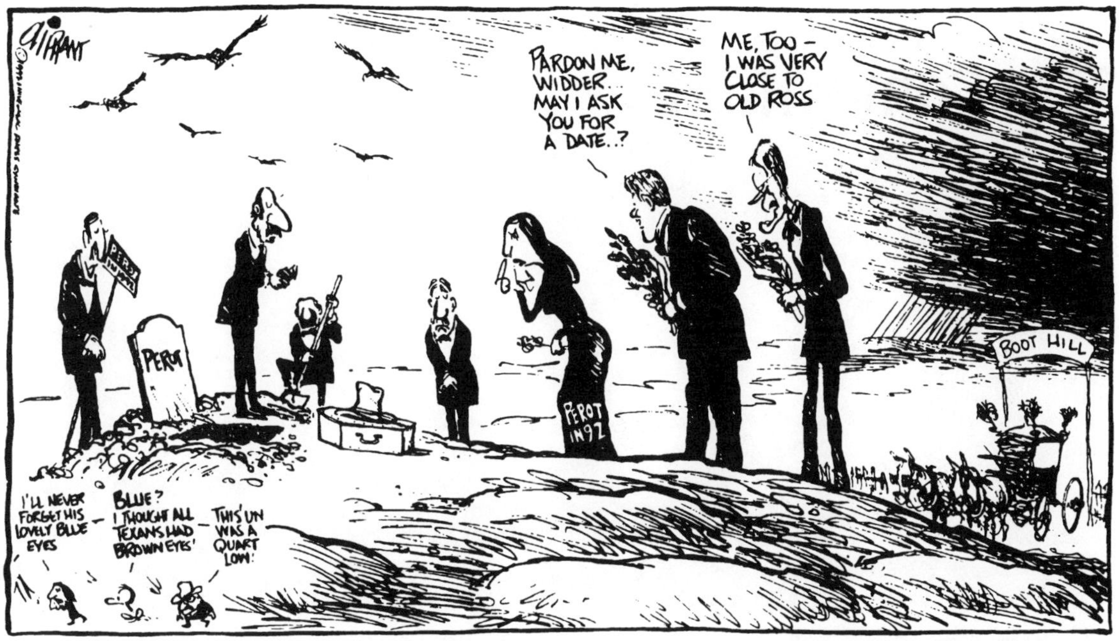
PARDON ME, WIDDER.. MAY I ASK YOU FOR A DATE..?
ME, TOO - I WAS VERY CLOSE TO OLD ROSS
PEROT
PEROT IN 92
BOOT HILL
I'LL NEVER FORGET HIS LOVELY BLUE EYES
BLUE? I THOUGHT ALL TEXANS HAD BROWN EYES'
THIS'UN WAS A QUART LOW!

The Convention

Ed Gamble

Concerns that Gore would overshadow Clinton continued at the convention.

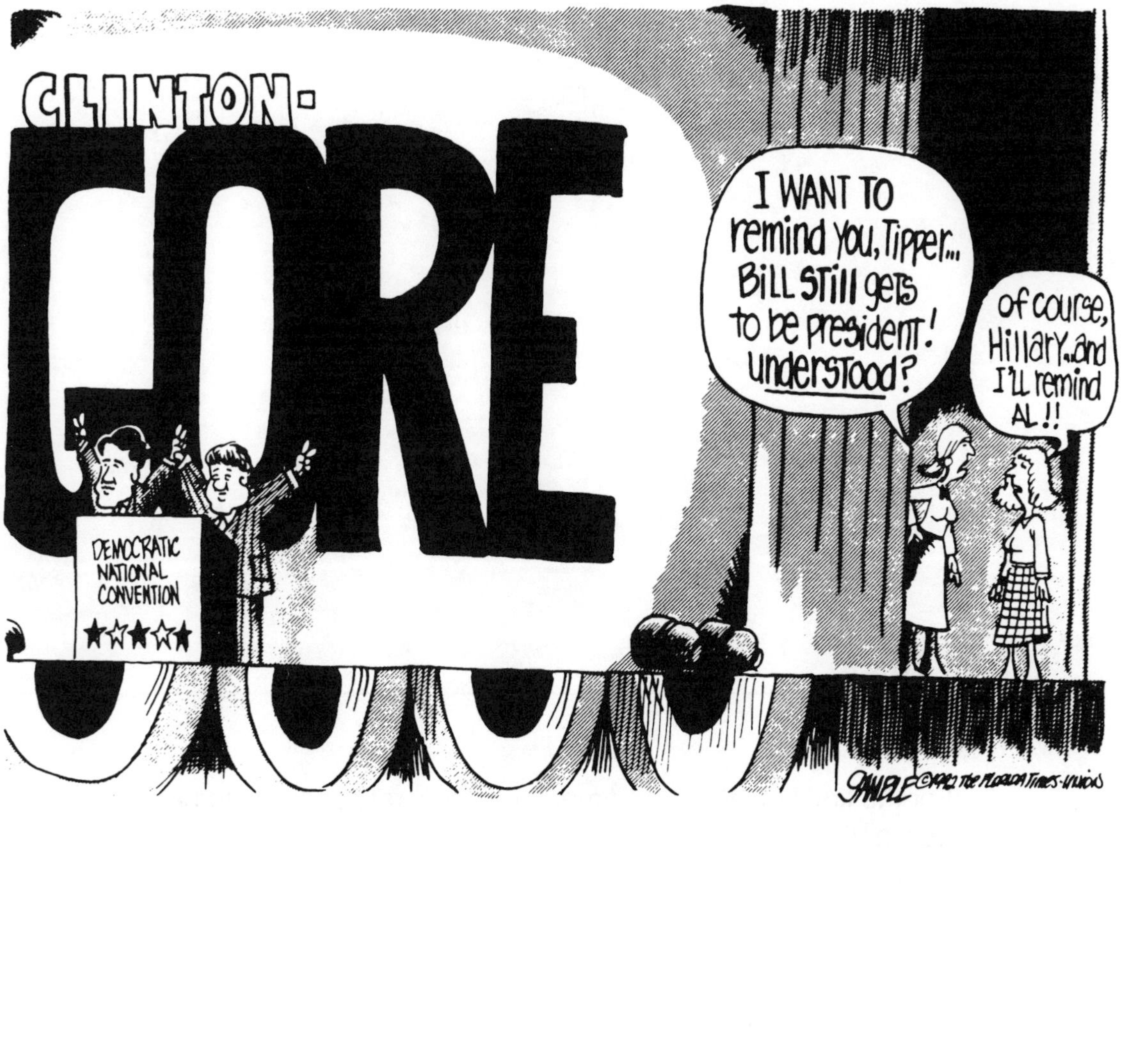
CLINTON-
GORE
DEMOCRATIC NATIONAL CONVENTION
I WANT TO remind you, Tipper... BILL STILL gets to be president! understood?
of course, Hillary.. and I'LL remind AL!!
©1992 The Florida Times-Union

Tom Toles

For the first time in a long time, the Democrats seemed to be nominating someone who had a real chance of winning the White House.

Tom Toles in *The Buffalo News*

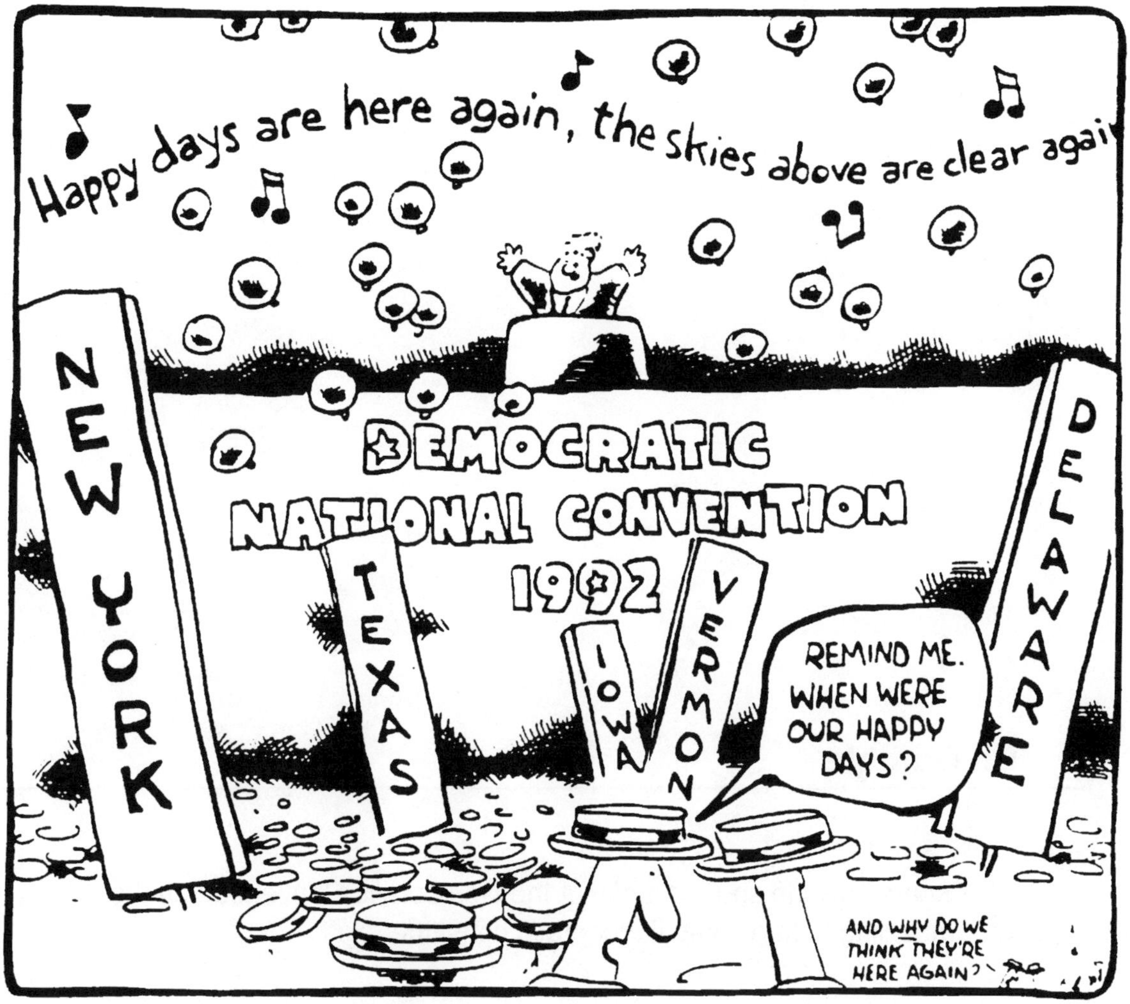
Happy days are here again, the skies above are clear agai
DEMOCRATIC NATIONAL CONVENTION 1992
NEW YORK
TEXAS
IOWA
VERMON
DELAWARE
REMIND ME. WHEN WERE OUR HAPPY DAYS?
AND WHY DO WE THINK THEY'RE HERE AGAIN?

Ed Gamble

Some saw the show of unity at the Democratic Convention as the muzzling of traditional Democratic constituencies.

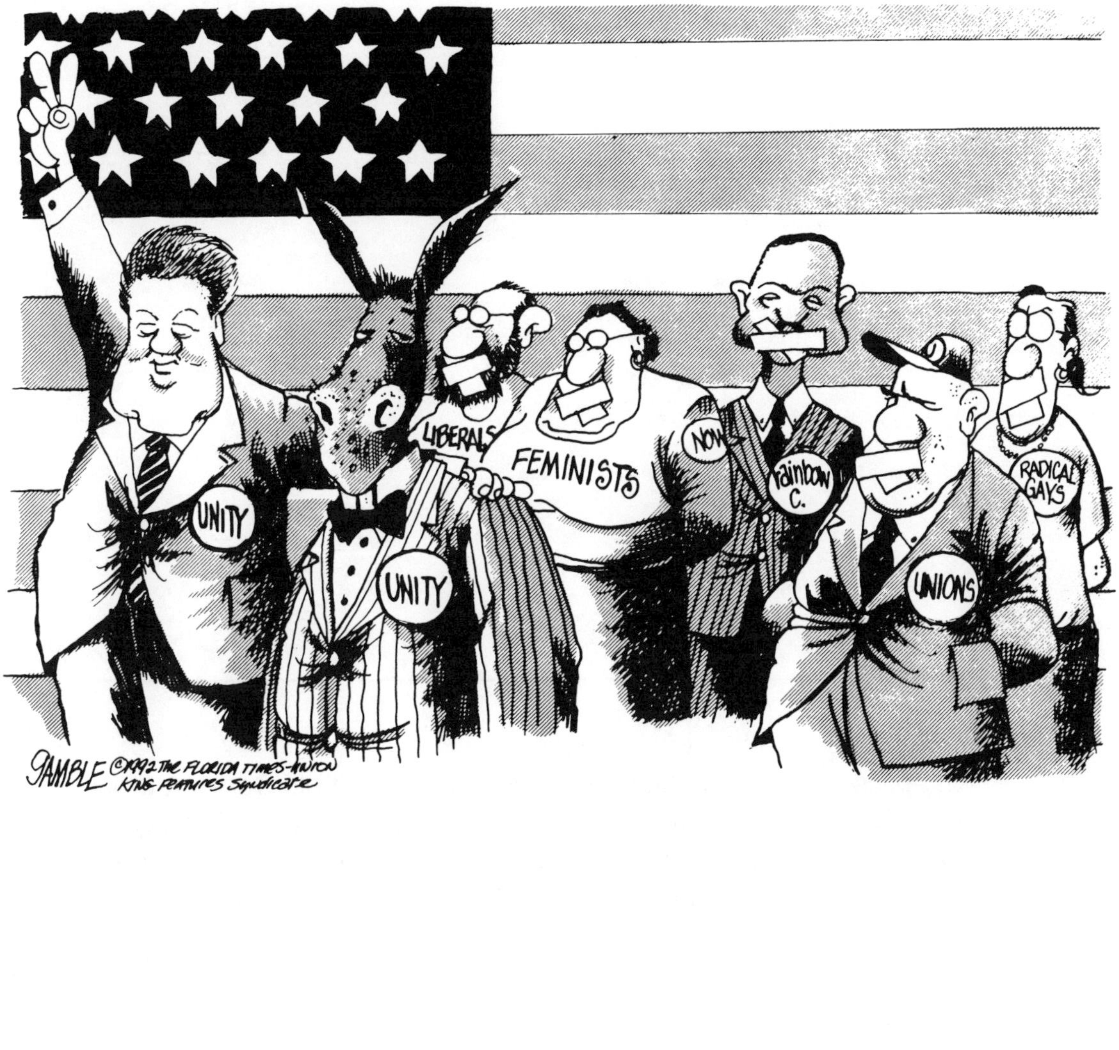

UNITY
UNITY
LIBERALS
FEMINISTS
NOW
rainbow C.
UNIONS
RADICAL GAYS
GAMBLE ©1992 The Florida Times-Union
King Features Syndicate

Henry Payne

Skeptics wondered if the new Democrats weren't old Democrats in moderate clothing. Party old-timer George McGovern, an old-style Liberal, described the Trojan horse idea in an interview during the campaign. Clinton had worked on McGovern's presidential campaign in 1972.

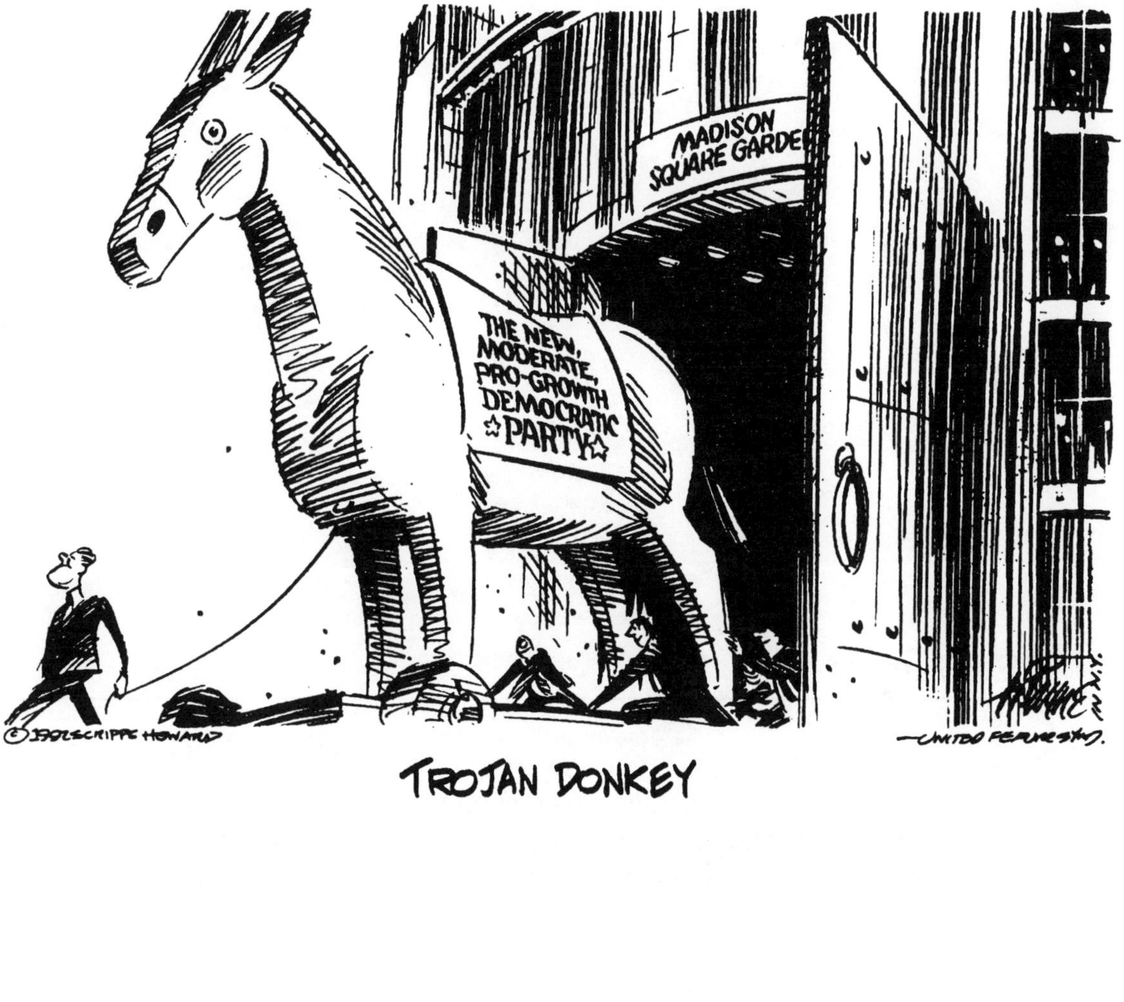
MADISON SQUARE GARDE
THE NEW, MODERATE, PRO-GROWTH DEMOCRATIC PARTY

TROJAN DONKEY

Ed Gamble

The end of the Democratic Convention focused attention on the Bush-Clinton contest to come. Republicans prepared to harp on Clinton's so-called personal issues; Clinton prepared to zero in on Bush's handling of the economy and his "No new taxes" pledge.

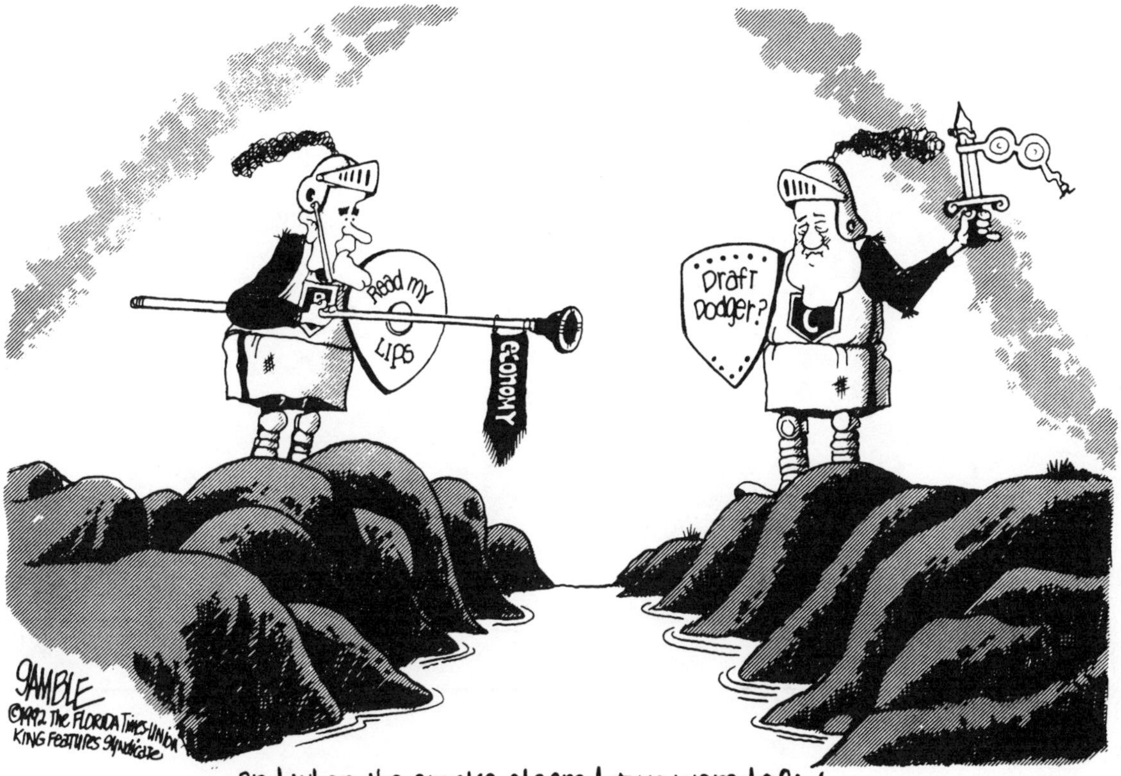
Read my
LIPS
ECONOMY
Draft Dodger?
GAMBLE
©1992 The FLORIDA Times-Union
KING Features Syndicate

...and when the smoke cleared, two were Left!

Ed Gamble

The convention gave Clinton a twenty-plus point bounce in the polls, but the candidate remembered full well what had happened to the last Democrat to experience a similar surge.

Reprinted with special permission of King Features Syndicate

Back into the Fray

Mike Luckovich

Clinton may have been cleaned up and dressed as a new Democrat, but the Republicans were threatening to dump mud all over his campaign.

Creators Syndicate

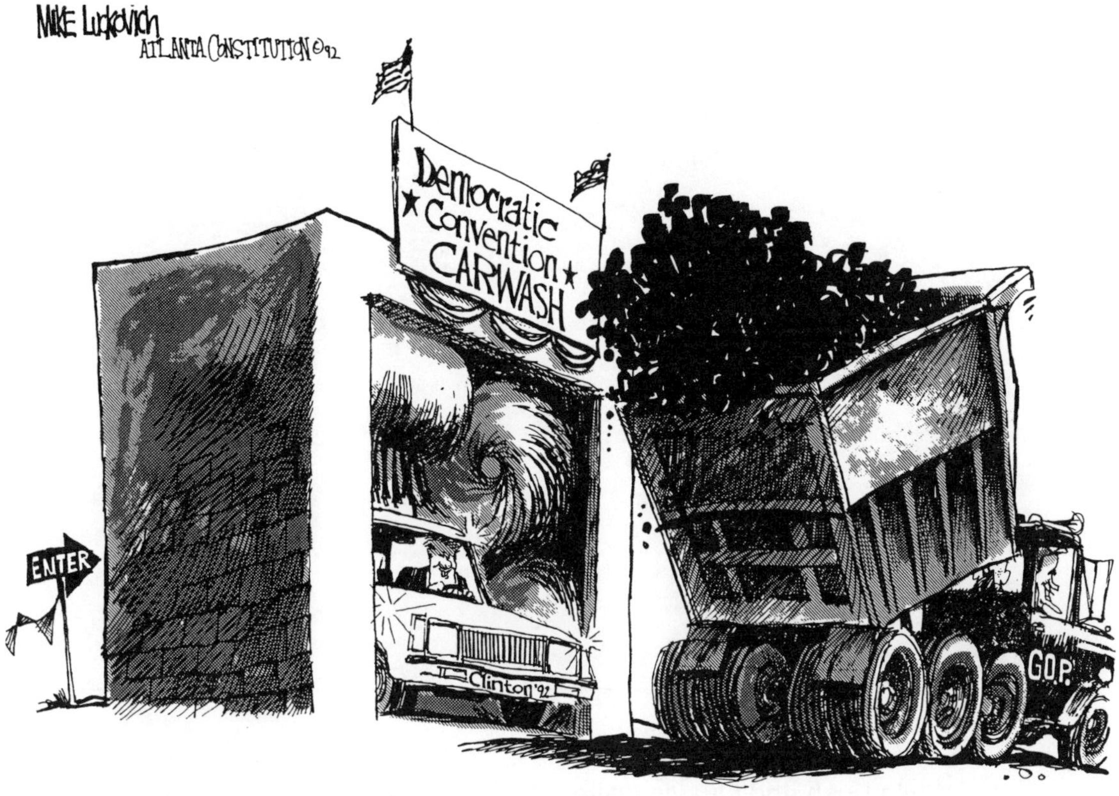
MIKE Luckovich
ATLANTA CONSTITUTION ©92
Democratic
★ Convention
CARWASH ★
ENTER
Clinton '92
G.O.P.

Jim Borgman

While Bush and Quayle waited until after the GOP convention to start their campaign, Bill and Al and Hillary and Tipper embarked on a bus tour immediately after the convention. The '92 tour proved popular with voters and was made for TV. Small-town newspapers provided tons of coverage.

Reprinted with special permission of King Features Syndicate

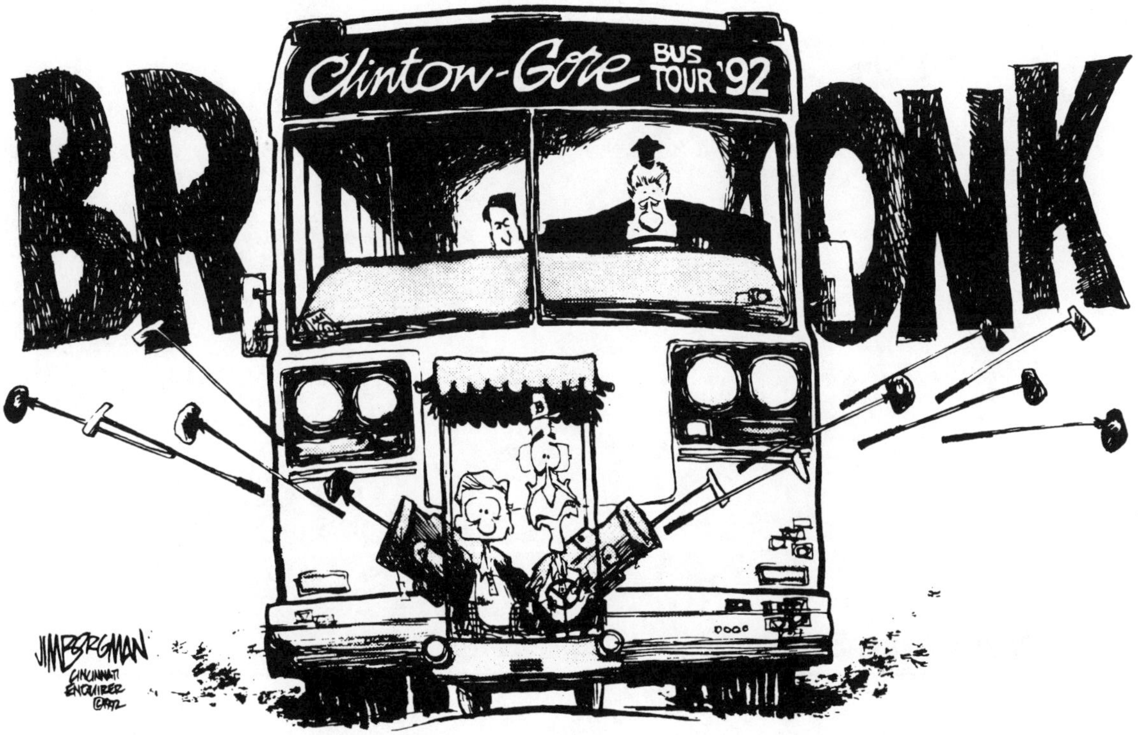
Clinton-Gore BUS TOUR '92
BR
ONK
JIM BORGMAN
CINCINNATI ENQUIRER
©1992

Mark Alan Stamaty

Two policy wonks on the loose. Outsiders were left to wonder about the conversations between Clinton and Gore during the bus trips.

Mark Alan Stamaty, *The Village Voice*

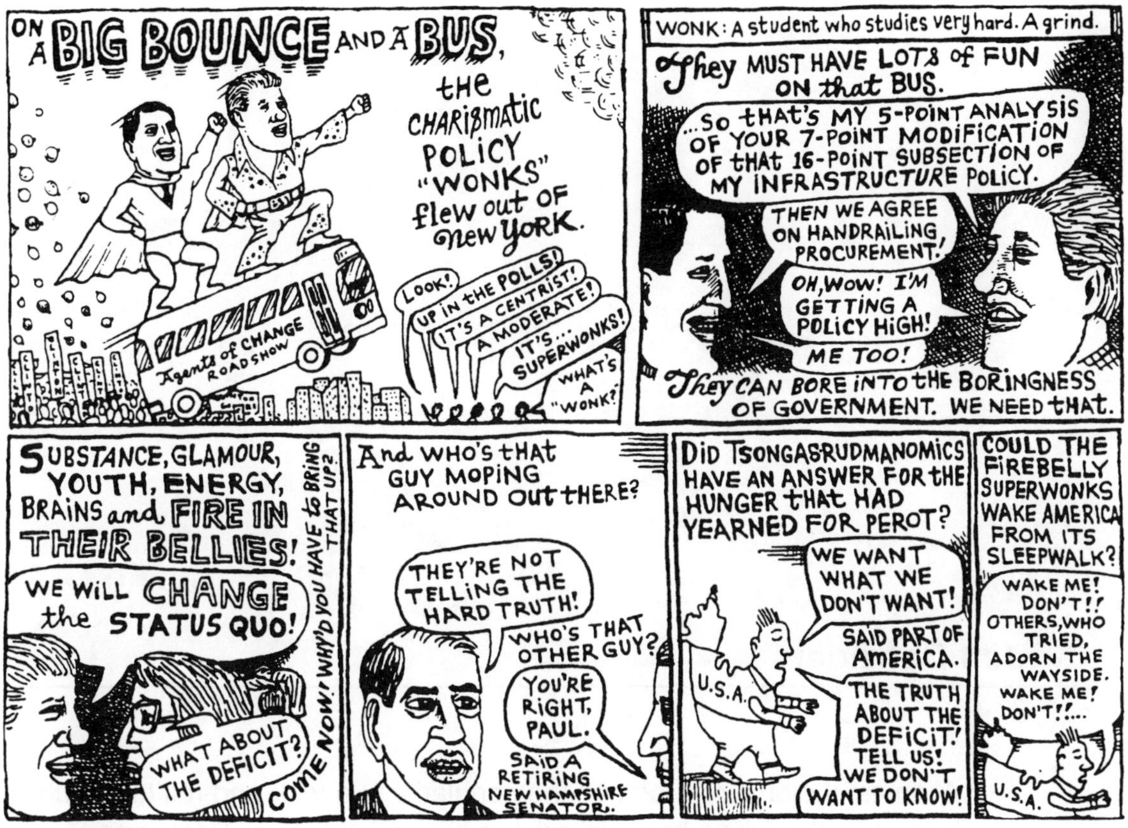

ON A BIG BOUNCE AND A BUS,
the CHARISMATIC POLICY "WONKS" flew out of New YORK.
Agents of CHANGE ROADSHOW
LOOK!
UP IN THE POLLS!
IT'S A CENTRIST!
A MODERATE!
IT'S... SUPERWONKS!
WHAT'S A "WONK?"
WONK: A student who studies very hard. A grind.
They MUST HAVE LOTS OF FUN ON that BUS.
...SO THAT'S MY 5-POINT ANALYSIS OF YOUR 7-POINT MODIFICATION OF THAT 16-POINT SUBSECTION OF MY INFRASTRUCTURE POLICY.
THEN WE AGREE ON HANDRAILING PROCUREMENT!
OH, WOW! I'M GETTING A POLICY HIGH!
ME TOO!
They CAN BORE INTO THE BORINGNESS OF GOVERNMENT. WE NEED THAT.
SUBSTANCE, GLAMOUR, YOUTH, ENERGY, BRAINS and FIRE IN THEIR BELLIES!
WE WILL CHANGE the STATUS QUO!
WHAT ABOUT THE DEFICIT?
COME NOW! WHY'D YOU HAVE to BRING THAT UP?
And WHO'S THAT GUY MOPING AROUND OUT THERE?
THEY'RE NOT TELLING THE HARD TRUTH!
WHO'S THAT OTHER GUY?
YOU'RE RIGHT, PAUL.
SAID A RETIRING NEW HAMPSHIRE SENATOR.
DID TSONGASRUDMANOMICS HAVE AN ANSWER FOR THE HUNGER THAT HAD YEARNED FOR PEROT?
WE WANT WHAT WE DON'T WANT!
SAID PART OF AMERICA.
U.S.A.
THE TRUTH ABOUT THE DEFICIT! TELL US! WE DON'T WANT TO KNOW!
COULD THE FIREBELLY SUPERWONKS WAKE AMERICA FROM ITS SLEEPWALK?
WAKE ME! DON'T!! OTHERS, WHO TRIED, ADORN THE WAYSIDE. WAKE ME! DON'T!!...
U.S.A.

Jeff Danziger

At times, the bus trips took on the popularity of a rock-and-roll tour, with huge crowds waiting hours to catch a glimpse of the candidates and their wives. Comparisons between Clinton and his music idol, Elvis, continued throughout the campaign.

Danziger in *The Christian Science Monitor* ©1992 TCSPS

FOR THE LAST TIME ... YOU DID NOT SEE ELVIS!
ELVIS AIN'T GONNA COME RIDIN' THROUGH ON A BUS...
WEIRD Romance

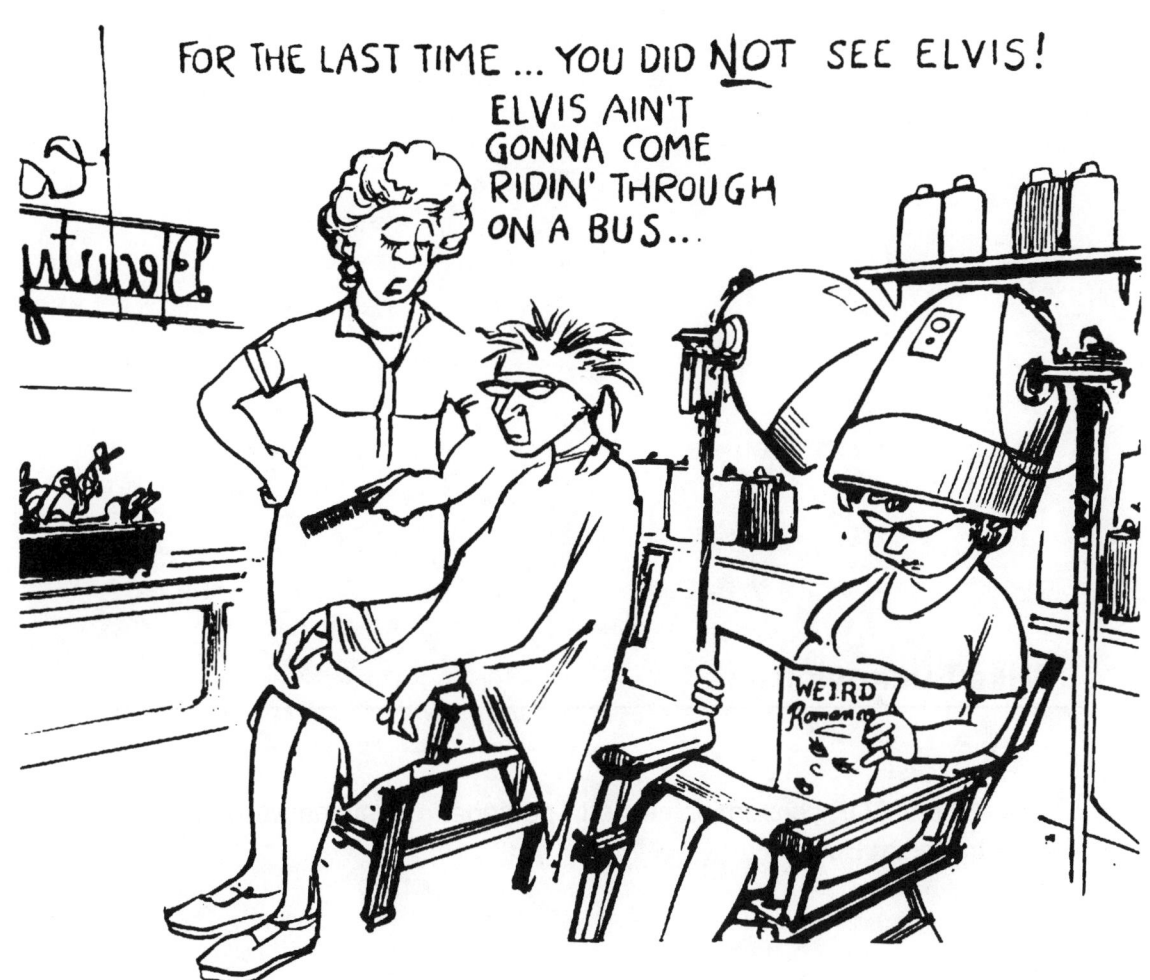

Mike Luckovich

As the GOP convention neared, "personal" questions were now being hurled at Bush.

Creators Syndicate

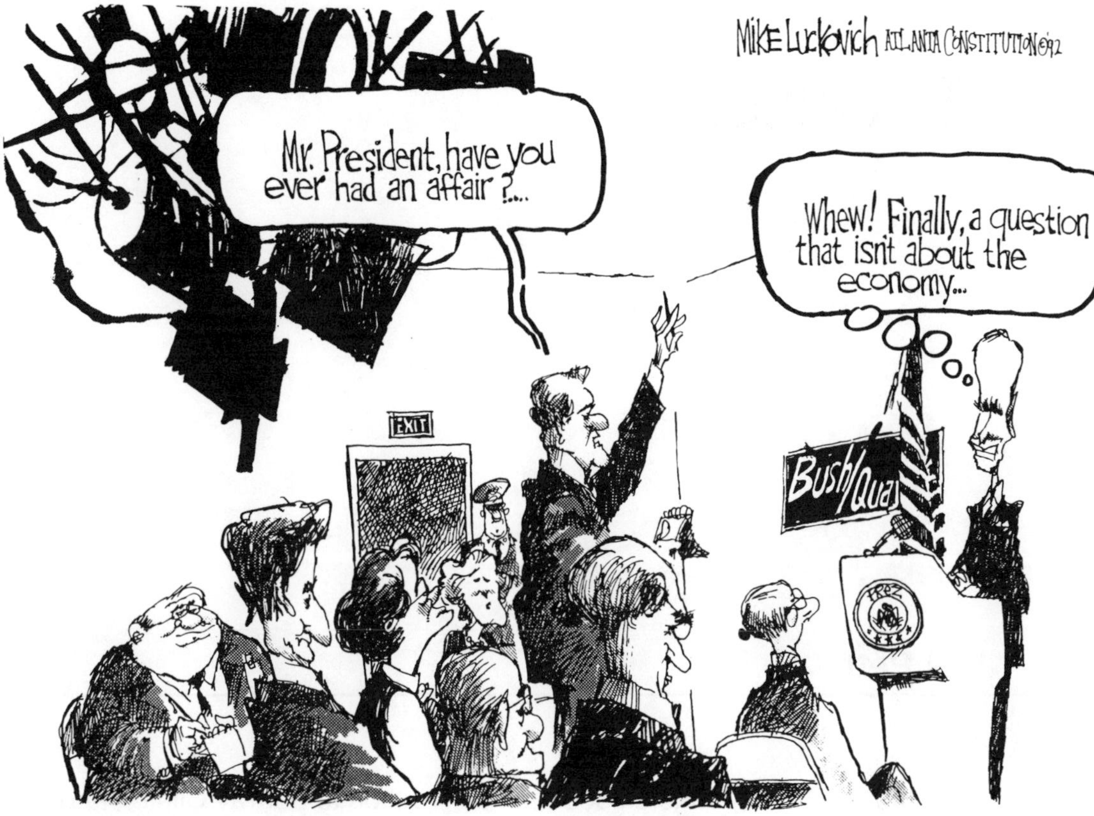
MIKE LUCKOVICH ATLANTA CONSTITUTION ©92
Mr. President, have you ever had an affair ?...
Whew! Finally, a question that isn't about the economy...
EXIT
Bush/Quay

Family Values

Joel Pett

Strident GOP speakers used their convention to portray Clinton and the Democrats as being not in tune with "family values."

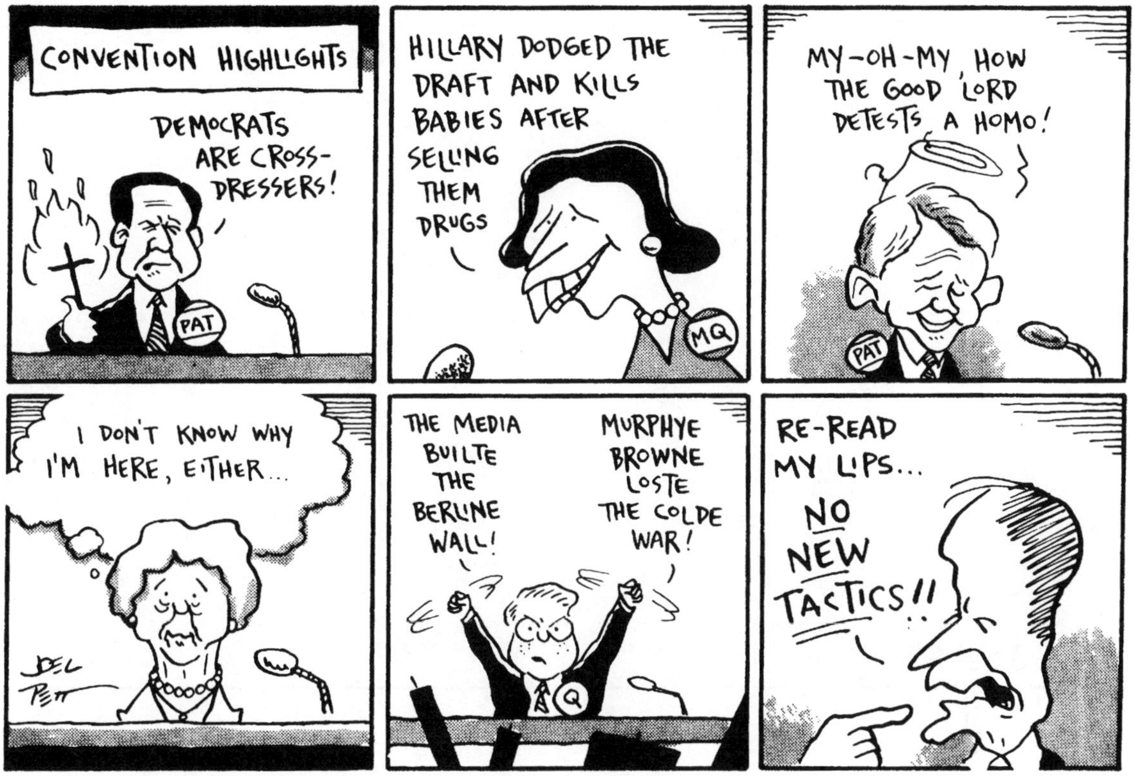
CONVENTION HIGHLIGHTS
DEMOCRATS ARE CROSS-DRESSERS!
PAT
HILLARY DODGED THE DRAFT AND KILLS BABIES AFTER SELLING THEM DRUGS
MQ
MY-OH-MY, HOW THE GOOD LORD DETESTS A HOMO!
PAT
I DON'T KNOW WHY I'M HERE, EITHER...
JOEL PETT
THE MEDIA BUILTE THE BERLINE WALL!
MURPHYE BROWNE LOSTE THE COLDE WAR!
Q
RE-READ MY LIPS...
NO NEW TACTICS!!

Joel Pett

From the White House, President Bush claimed that he was not interested in a mud-slinging campaign. But the tactics carried out by GOP operatives made some wonder. Actress Mia Farrow accused longtime companion Woody Allen of child abuse, a story made in tabloid heaven.

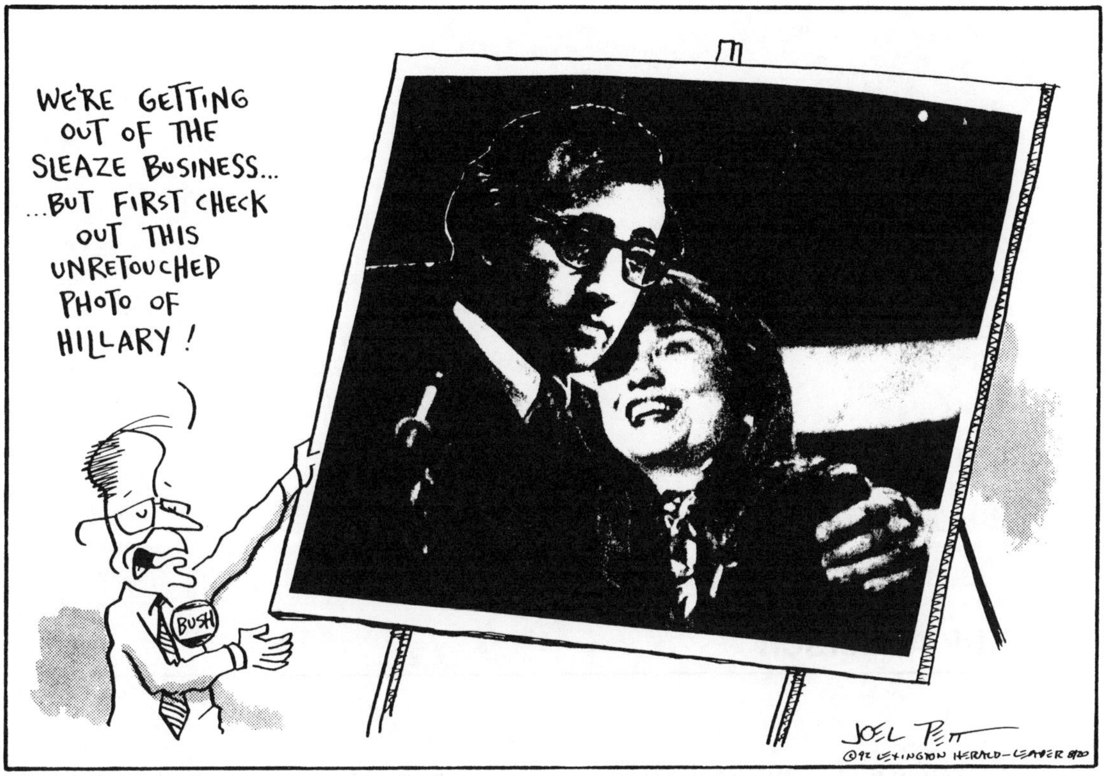
WE'RE GETTING OUT OF THE SLEAZE BUSINESS... ...BUT FIRST CHECK OUT THIS UNRETOUCHED PHOTO OF HILLARY!
BUSH
JOEL PETT
©92 LEXINGTON HERALD-LEADER 8/20

Kirk Anderson

Now that Republicans had raised the issue, Americans searched for a definition of "family values."

Kirk Anderson, Madison, WI

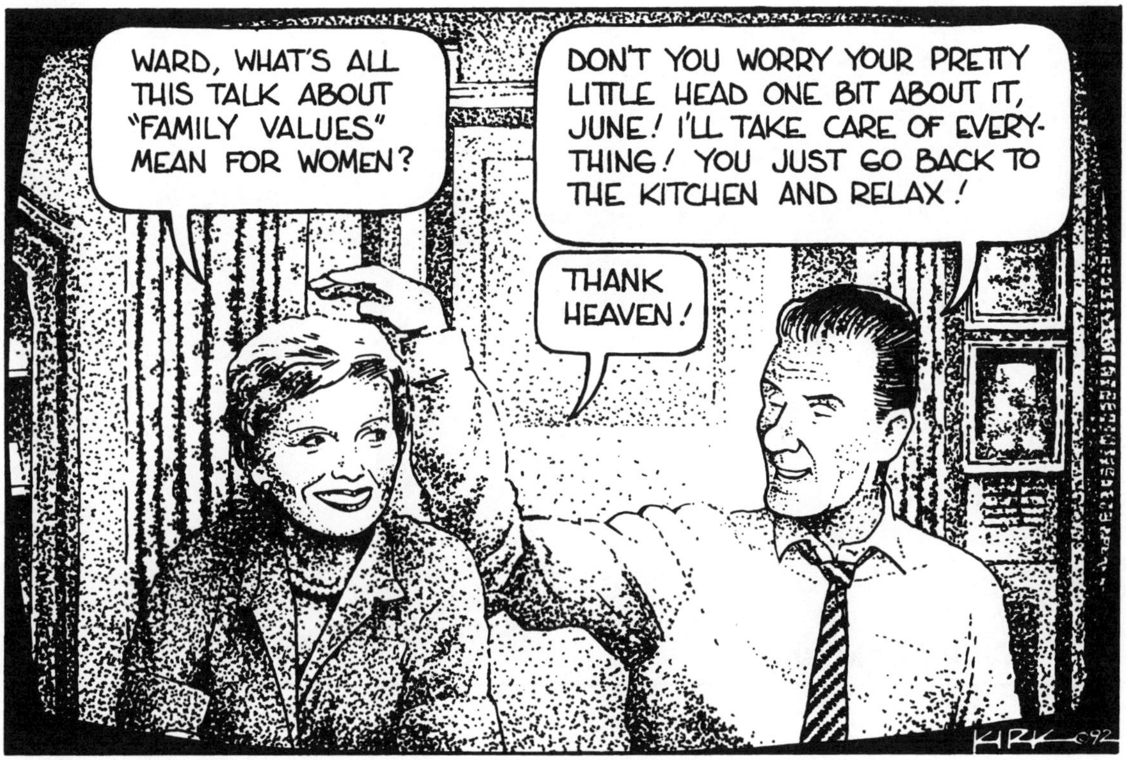
WARD, WHAT'S ALL THIS TALK ABOUT "FAMILY VALUES" MEAN FOR WOMEN?
DON'T YOU WORRY YOUR PRETTY LITTLE HEAD ONE BIT ABOUT IT, JUNE! I'LL TAKE CARE OF EVERY-THING! YOU JUST GO BACK TO THE KITCHEN AND RELAX!
THANK HEAVEN!

Mike Luckovich

The judgmental quality of the GOP convention frightened many.

Creators Syndicate

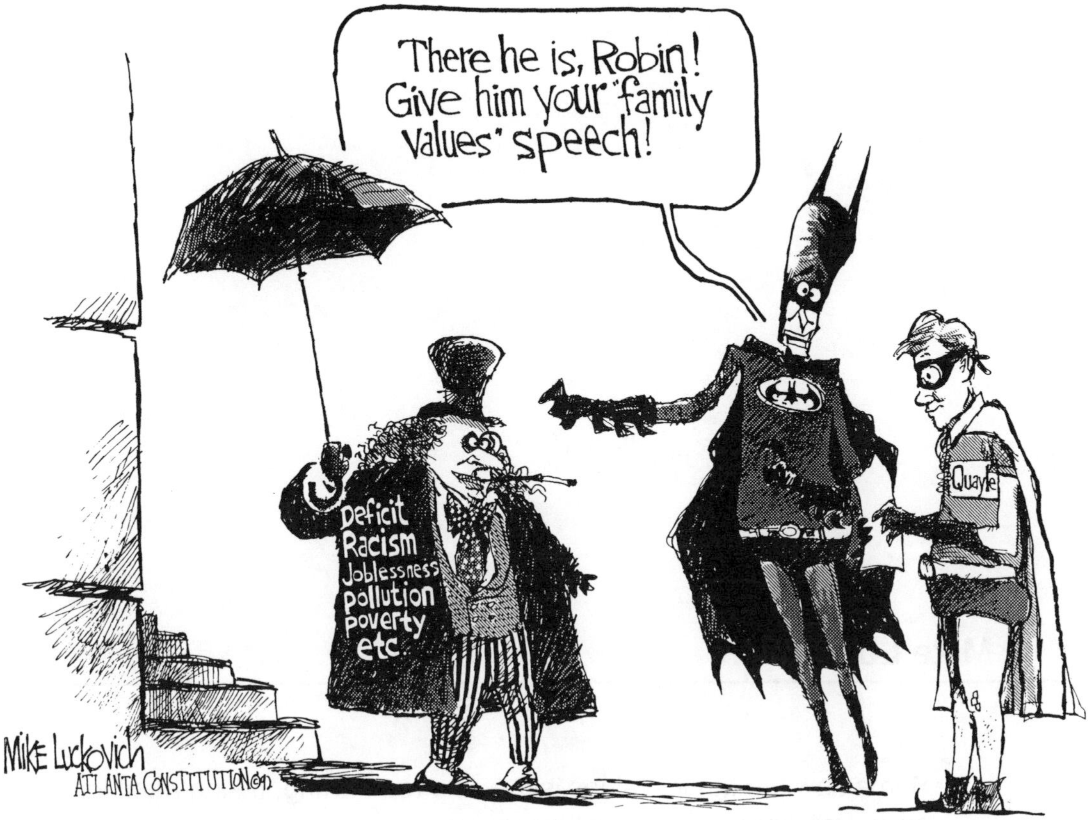
There he is, Robin! Give him your "family values" speech!
Deficit
Racism
Joblessness
pollution
poverty
etc.
Quayle
MIKE LUCKOVICH
ATLANTA CONSTITUTION ©92

Mike Luckovich

Some saw the family-values issue as a red herring, taking attention away from more critical problems.

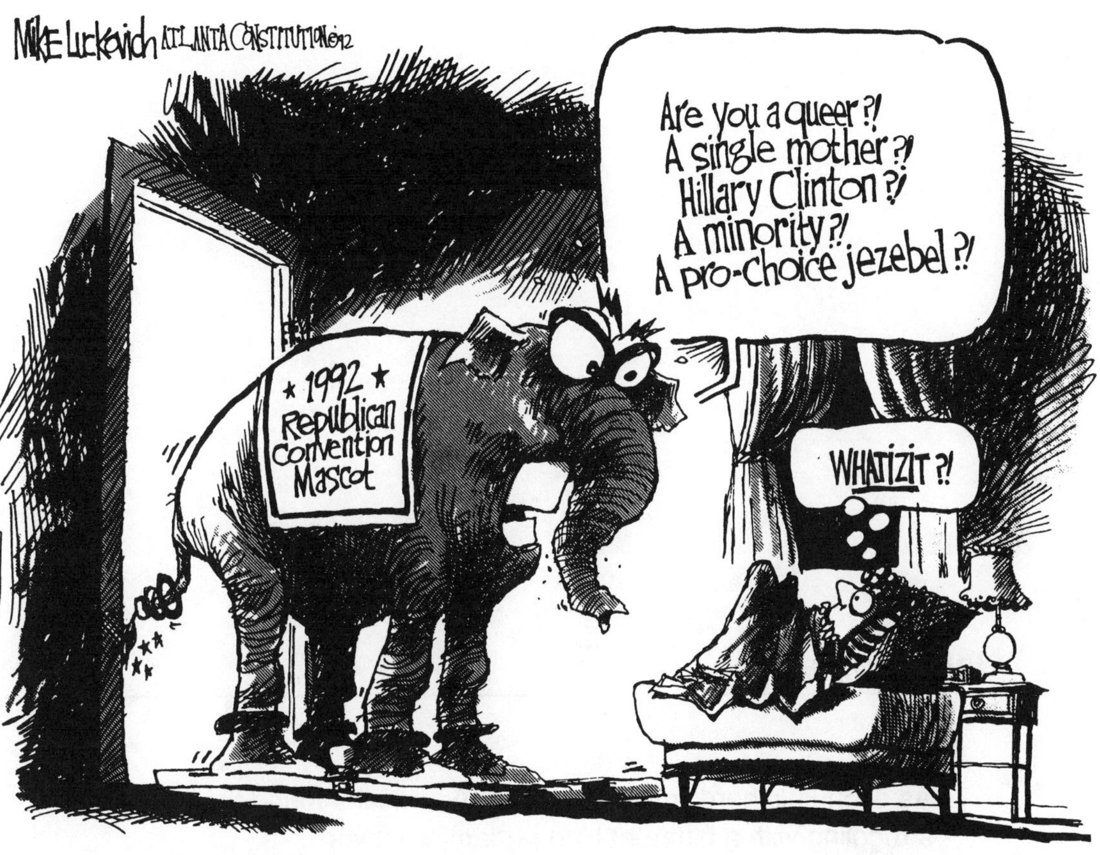
MIKE LUCKOVICH ATLANTA CONSTITUTION
Are you a queer?! A single mother?! Hillary Clinton?! A minority?! A pro-choice jezebel?!
★ 1992 ★ Republican Convention Mascot
WHATIZIT?!

Jack Ohman

As economic hard times continued, Americans found themselves struggling with a different kind of "family values."

The Oregonian. Tribune Media Services

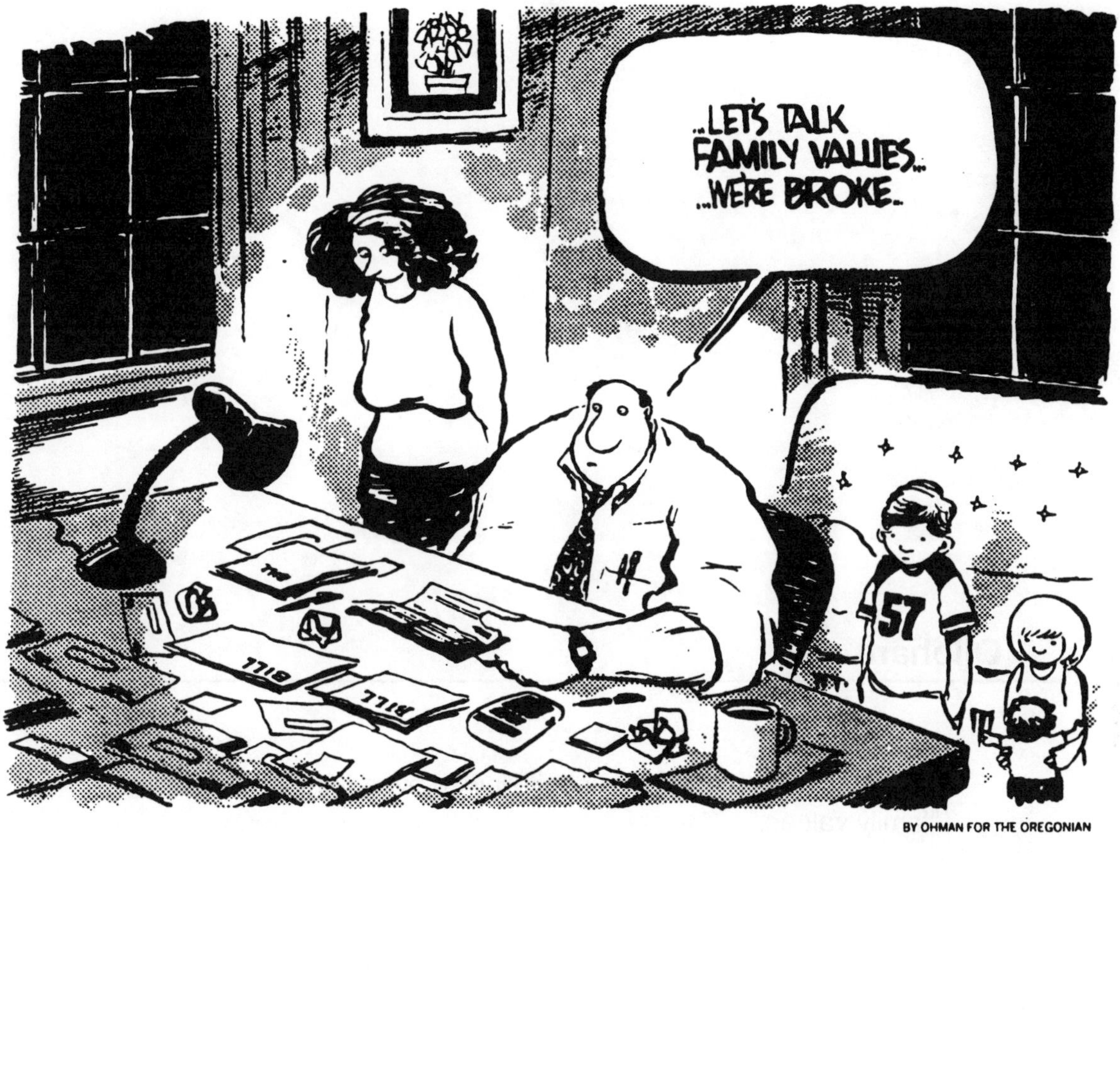
..LET'S TALK FAMILY VALUES...
...WE'RE BROKE..
BILL
BILL
BILL
57

BY OHMAN FOR THE OREGONIAN

Oliphant

At times, it seemed Republicans viewed everything as a matter of "family values."

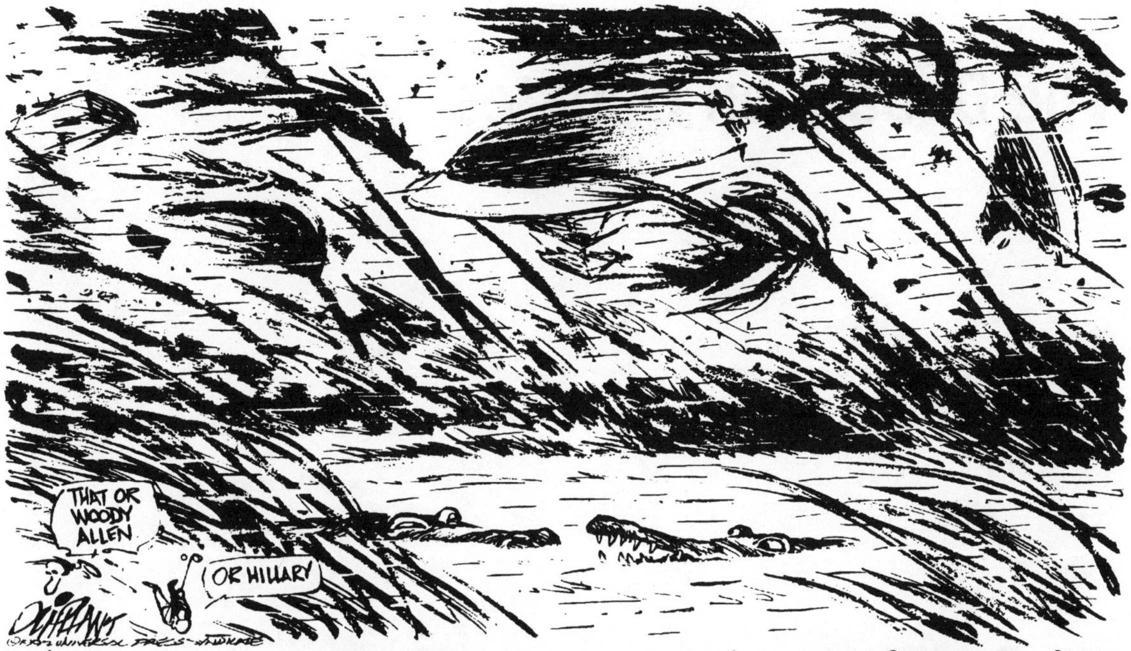
THAT OR WOODY ALLEN
OR HILLARY

'DON'T QUOTE ME ON THIS, BUT THESE HURRICANES ARE CAUSED BY GODLESS, NON-CHRISTIAN, PRO-CHOICE, ANTI-FAMILY, HOMOSEXUAL-SYMPATHIZING, LIBERAL, UNPATRIOTIC, PRO-CLINTON PREVERTS!'

The Debate on Debates

Don Wright

As the fall campaign got underway, Clinton had a hard time getting the Bush camp to agree to debates.

Don Wright, *The Palm Beach Post*

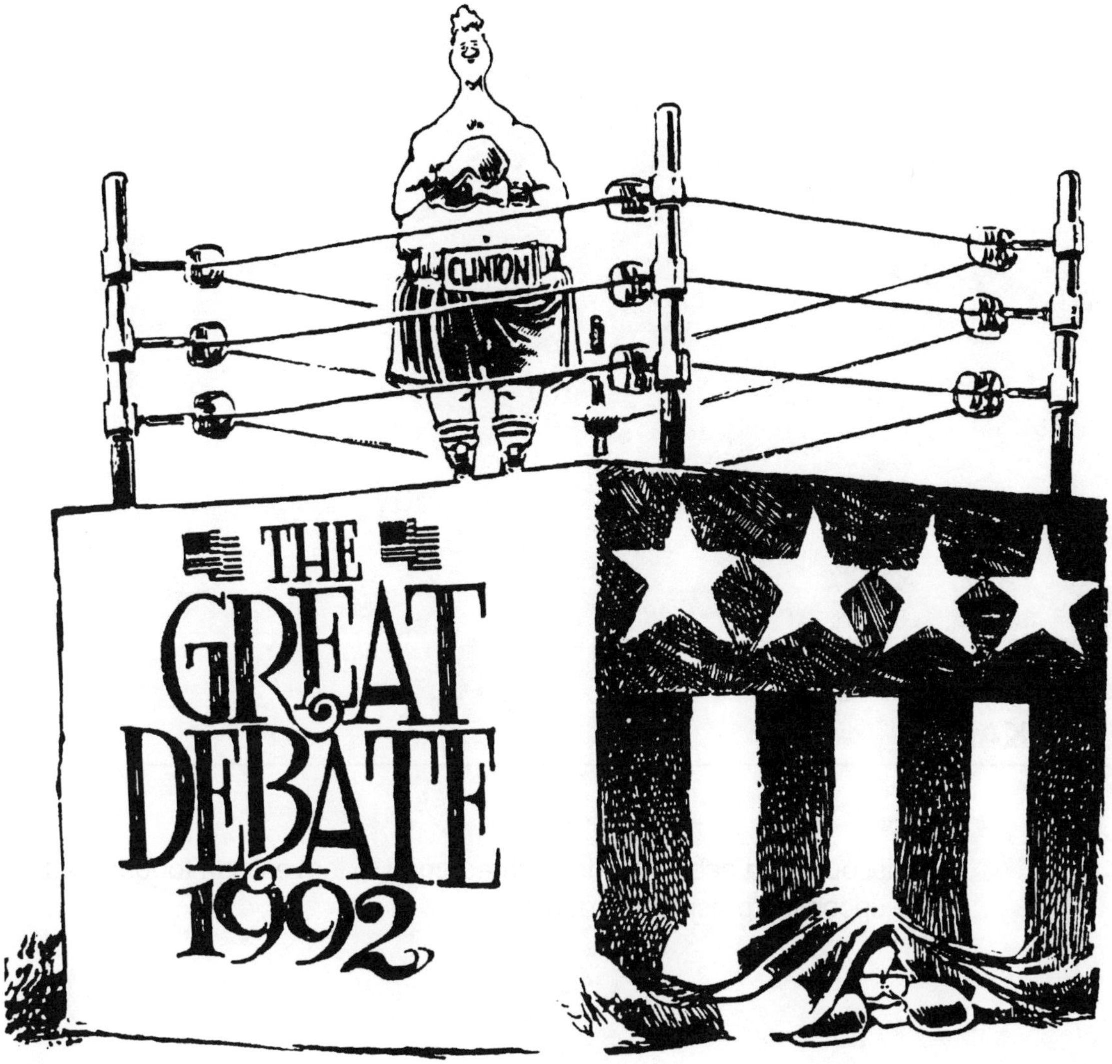
CLINTON
THE
GREAT
DEBATE
1992

KAL

Still-discouraging economic news threatened to leave Bush tongue-tied in the upcoming presidential debates.

Cartoonists and Writers Syndicate

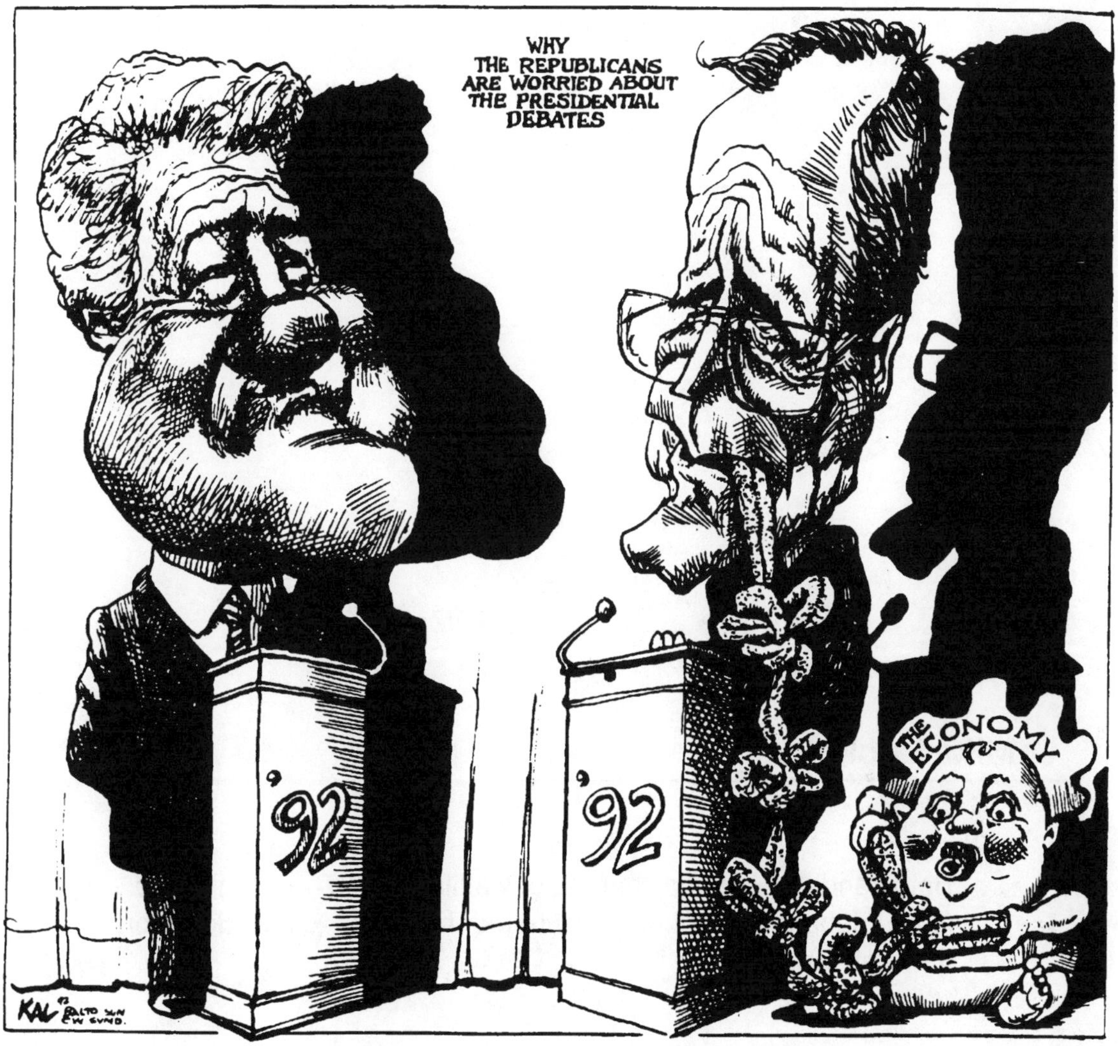
WHY
THE REPUBLICANS
ARE WORRIED ABOUT
THE PRESIDENTIAL
DEBATES
'92
'92
THE ECONOMY
KAL

Mike Luckovich

Both candidates faced charges of waffling: Bush on whether he would debate, and Clinton on whether he would "come clean" on the draft issue.

Creators Syndicate

It was a conflict I didn't want to be in. Frankly, I was worried about being wounded, or worse! So, I dodged it!...
...That doesn't mean I'm ruling out debates altogether...
MIKE LUCKOVICH ATLANTA CONSTITUTION

Dunagin

For the Bush camp, there was continuing concern about how the president's forensic abilities would match up with the articulate Arkansas governor.

Courtesy of *The Orlando Sentinel* and North America Syndicate Inc.

"YOU EXPECT ME TO DEBATE SOMEONE WHO COULD TALK HIMSELF OUT OF THE DRAFT?"

Tom Toles

The vice-presidential debate was expected to be an easy victory for Senator Gore, as pundits recalled Vice-President Quayle's problems against the 1988 Democratic vice-presidential nominee, Sen. Lloyd Bentsen of Texas.

Tom Toles in *The Buffalo News*

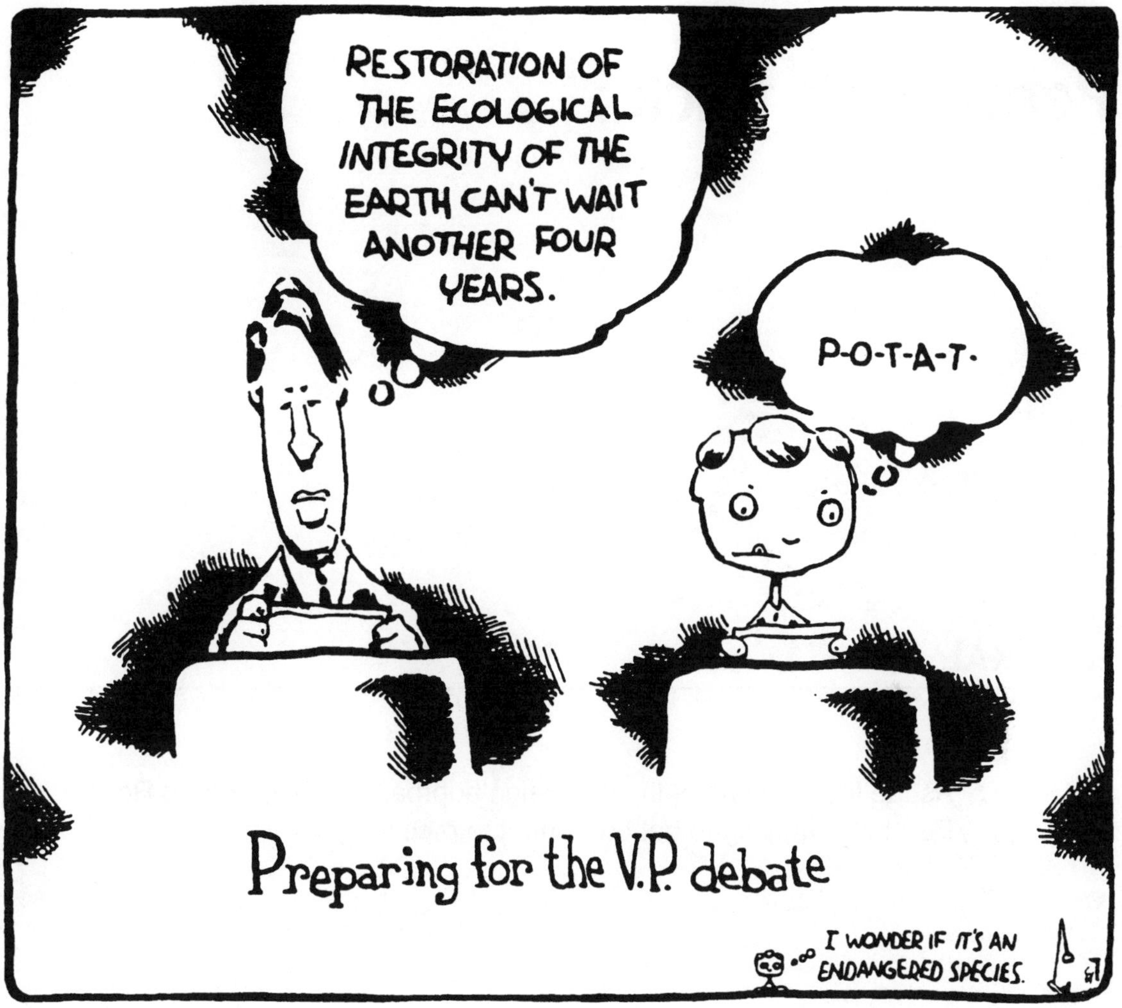
RESTORATION OF THE ECOLOGICAL INTEGRITY OF THE EARTH CAN'T WAIT ANOTHER FOUR YEARS.
P-O-T-A-T-
Preparing for the V.P. debate
I WONDER IF IT'S AN ENDANGERED SPECIES.

Perot: He's Back . . .

KAL

As the final months of the campaign approached, it appeared Ross Perot was angling to get back into the race.

Cartoonists and Writers Syndicate

152

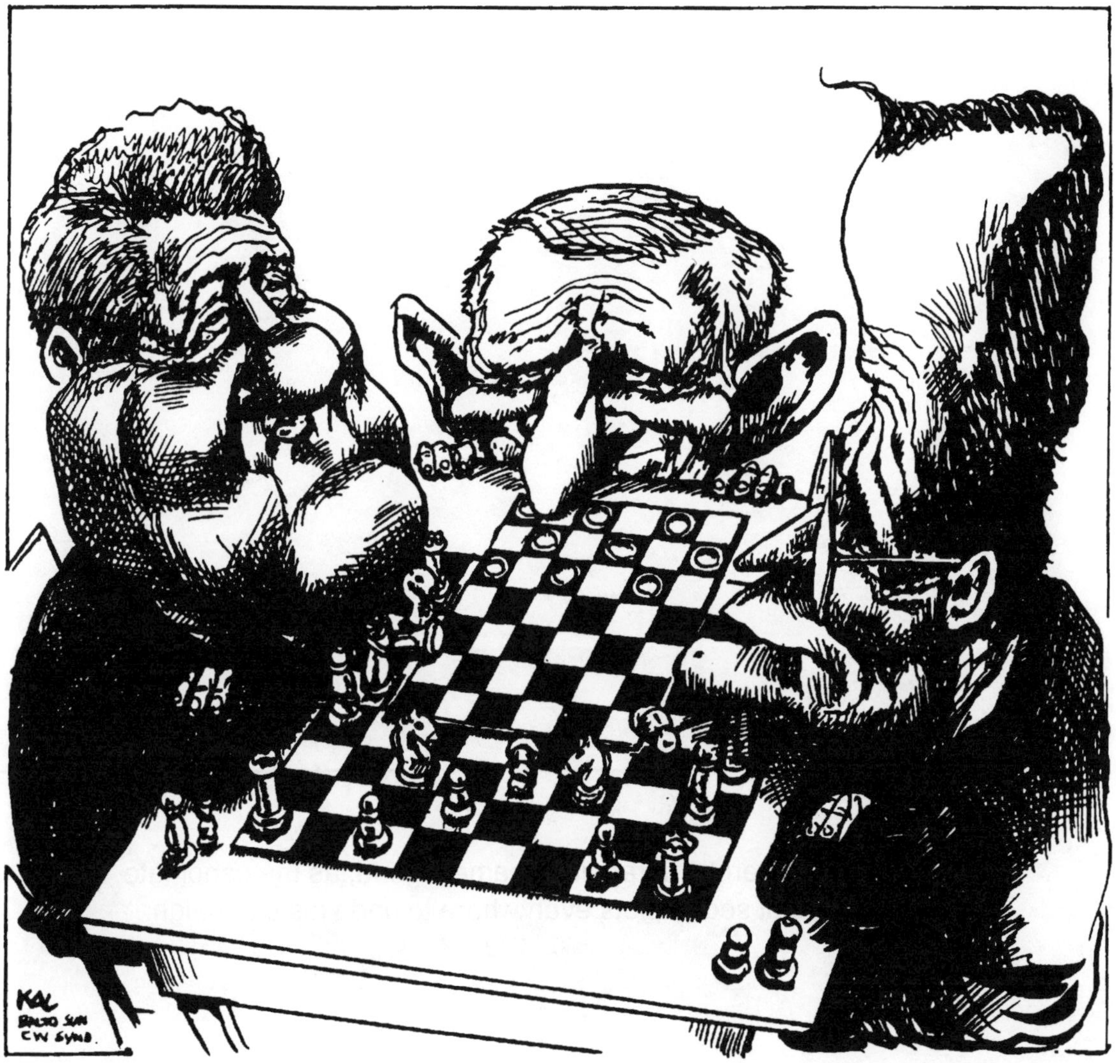
KAL
BALTO SUN
CW SYND.

Tom Toles

Stories about Perot's paranoia became legend, as the candidate seemed to spot secret plots everywhere to undo his campaign.

Tom Toles in *The Buffalo News*

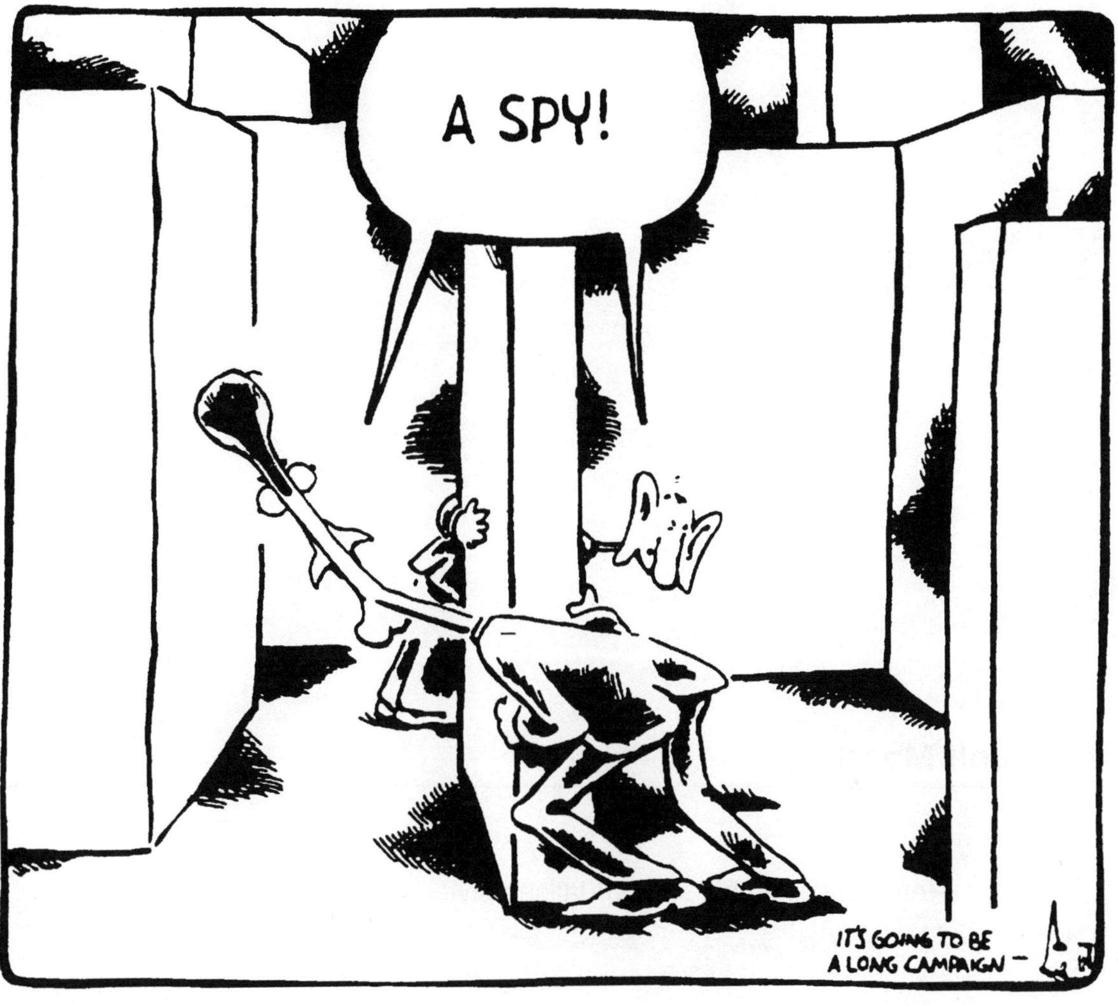
A SPY!
IT'S GOING TO BE
A LONG CAMPAIGN -

Jeff MacNelly

Perot fans liked his straight-talking style.

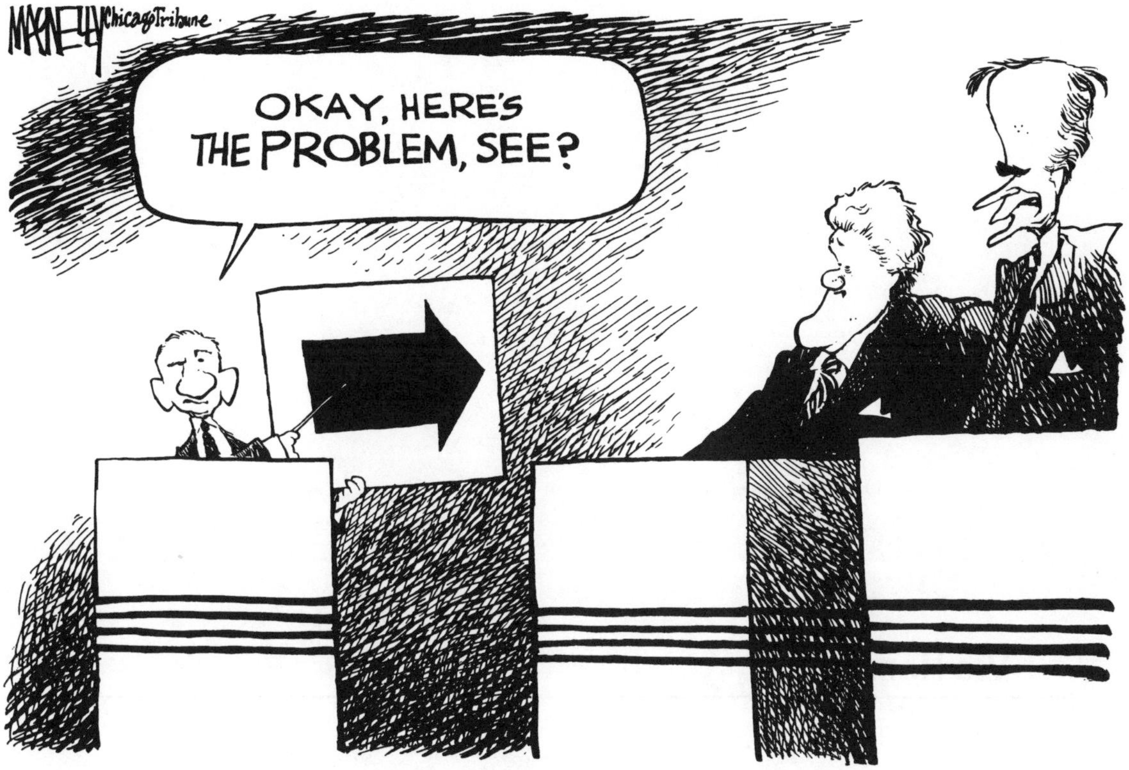
MAC NELLY Chicago Tribune
OKAY, HERE'S THE PROBLEM, SEE?

Vic Harville

Perot claimed his supporters would decide whether he got into the race, but many suspected otherwise.

Vic Harville/*Arkansas Democrat-Gazette*

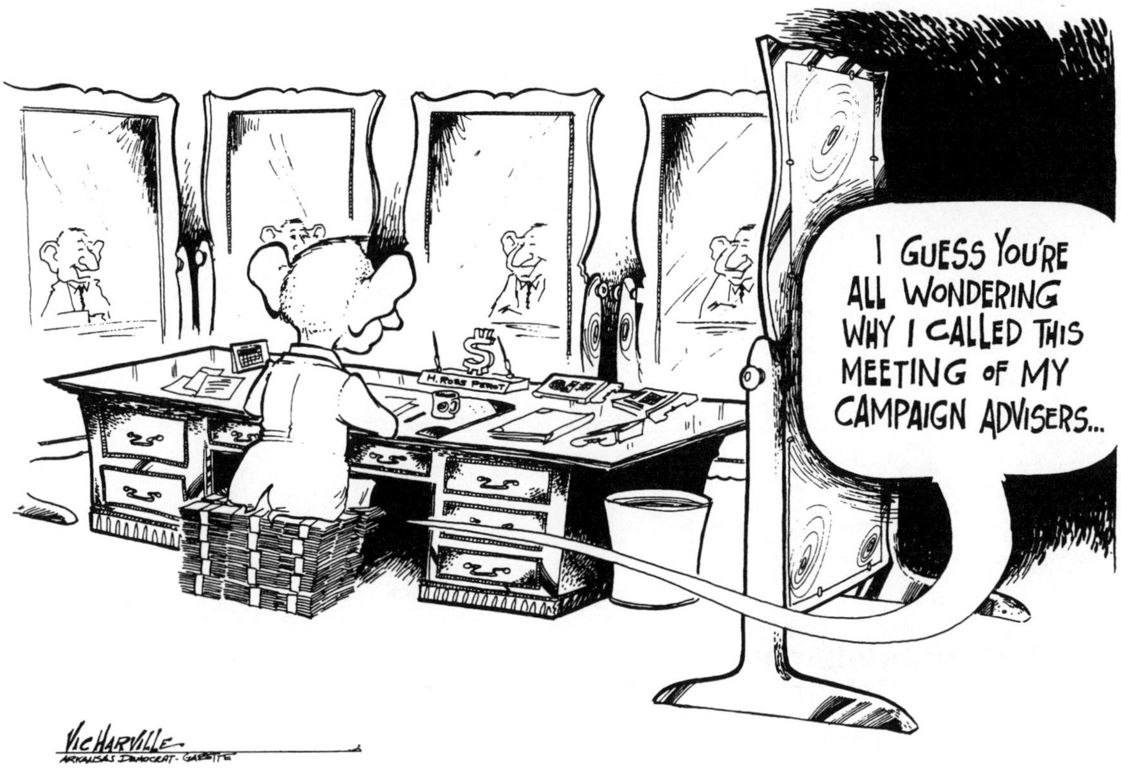
H. ROSS PEROT
I GUESS YOU'RE ALL WONDERING WHY I CALLED THIS MEETING OF MY CAMPAIGN ADVISERS...
VIC HARVILLE
ARKANSAS DEMOCRAT-GAZETTE

Hitting the Television Trail

J. B. Handelsman

Americans interpreted Bill Clinton's call for change in different ways.

"I didn't hear Bill Clinton say it was time for _me_ to change."

Chip Bok

Talk-show appearances became a key part of campaign strategy, as candidates tried to bypass the "filtering effect" of the conventional media.

By permission of Chip Bok and Creators Syndicate

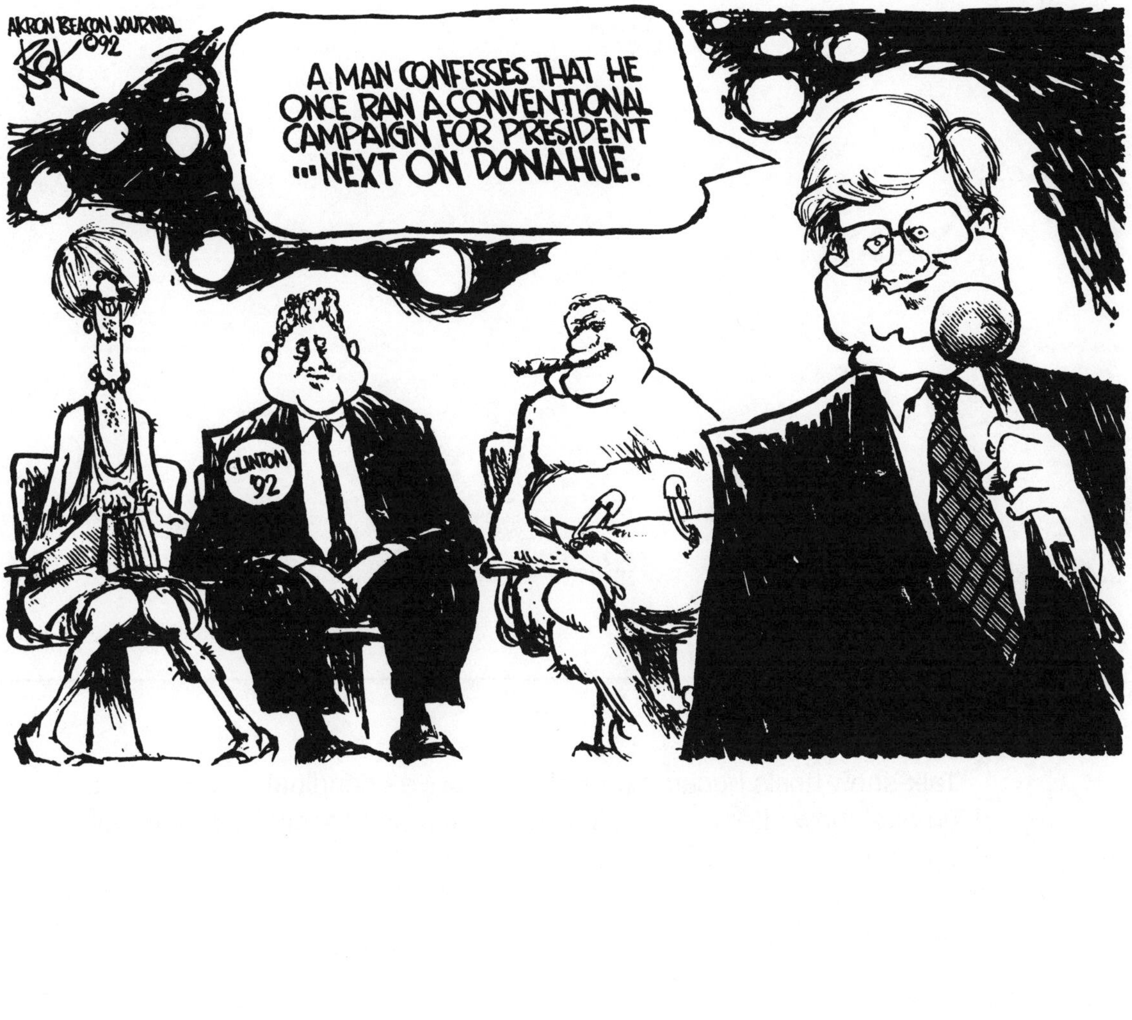
AKRON BEACON JOURNAL ©92
A MAN CONFESSES THAT HE ONCE RAN A CONVENTIONAL CAMPAIGN FOR PRESIDENT ...NEXT ON DONAHUE.
CLINTON '92

J. D. Crowe

Talk-show hosts became part of the news as candidates popped up
on one show after another, fielding what many considered "soft ball"
questions.

Courtesy of J. D. Crowe

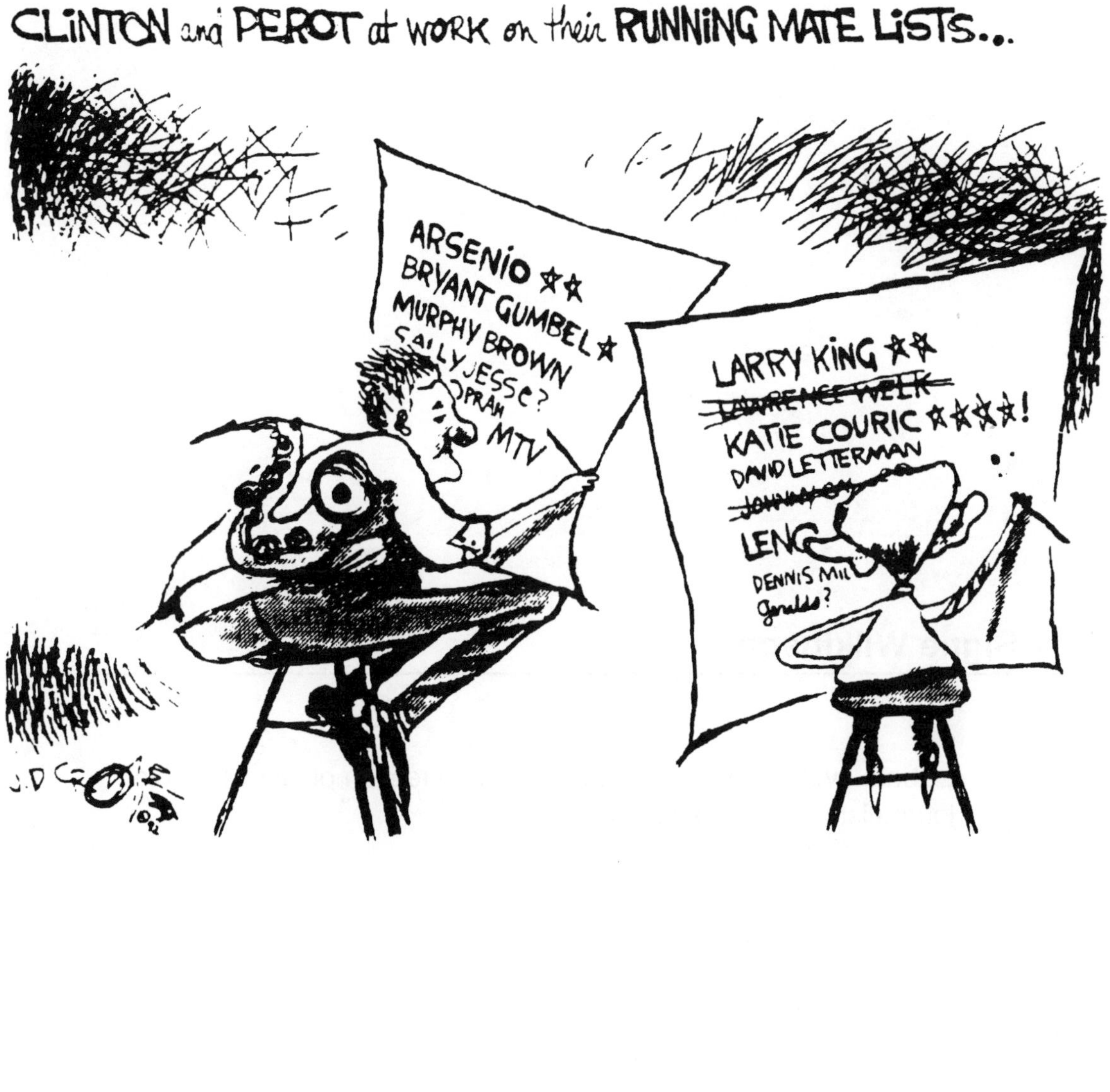
CLINTON and PEROT at WORK on their RUNNING MATE LISTS...
ARSENIO ☆☆
BRYANT GUMBEL ☆
MURPHY BROWN
SALLY JESSE?
OPRAH
MTV
LARRY KING ☆☆
LAWRENCE WELK
KATIE COURIC ☆☆☆☆!
DAVID LETTERMAN
LENO
DENNIS MIL
Geraldo?

Signe Wilkinson

Debate over debate formats raised the question of just what role journalists should play in the campaign.

Cartoonists and Writers Syndicate

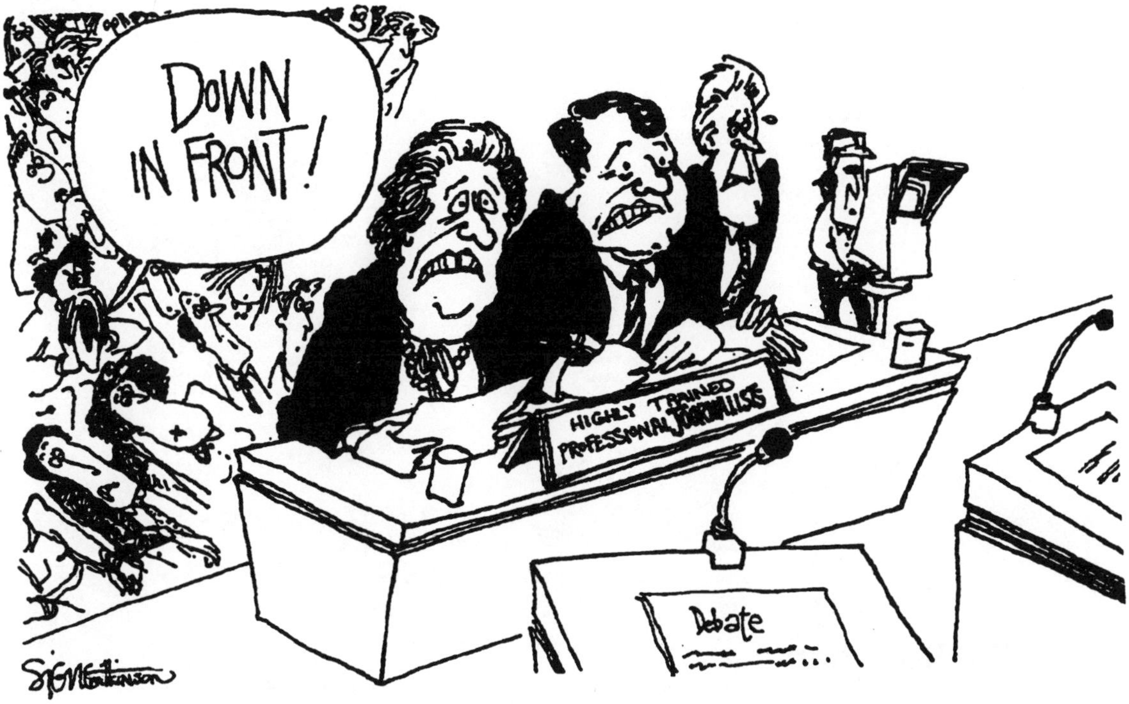
DOWN IN FRONT!
HIGHLY TRAINED PROFESSIONAL JOURNALISTS
Debate

Jim Borgman

Statements made on talk shows frequently became major
campaign news.

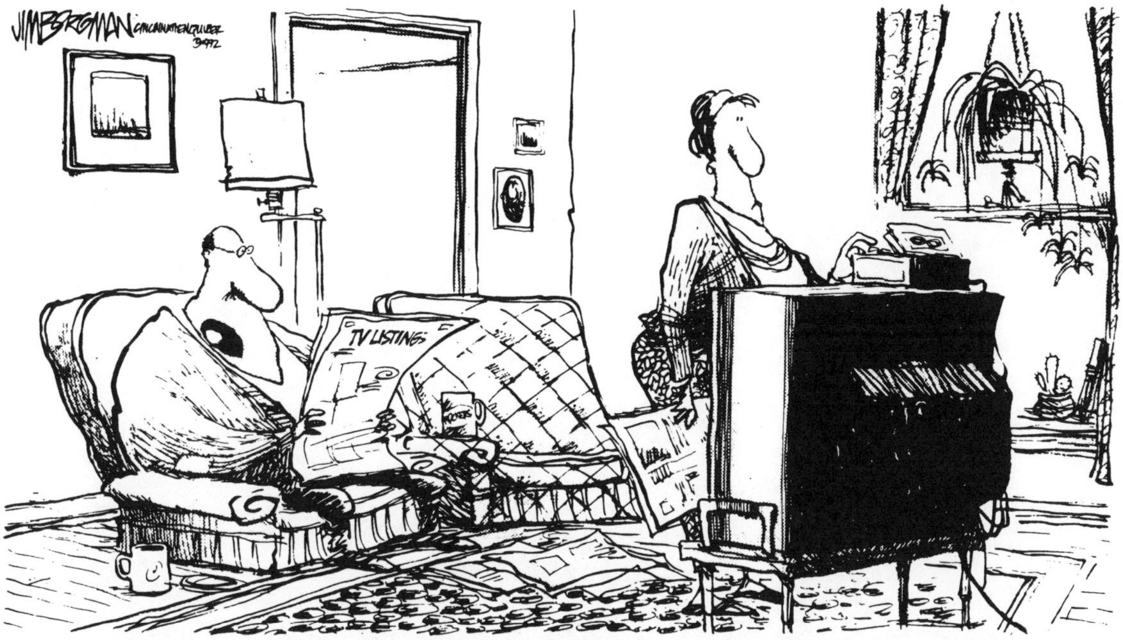
JIMBORGMAN
TV LISTINGS

"WE CAN WATCH CLINTON ON MTV, BUSH ON 'LETTERMAN', PEROT ON 'ARSENIO'..... OR MADONNA ON 'MEET THE PRESS'...."

Tom Meyer

Bush, who avoided the talk shows at first, began to play the talk-show game as well.

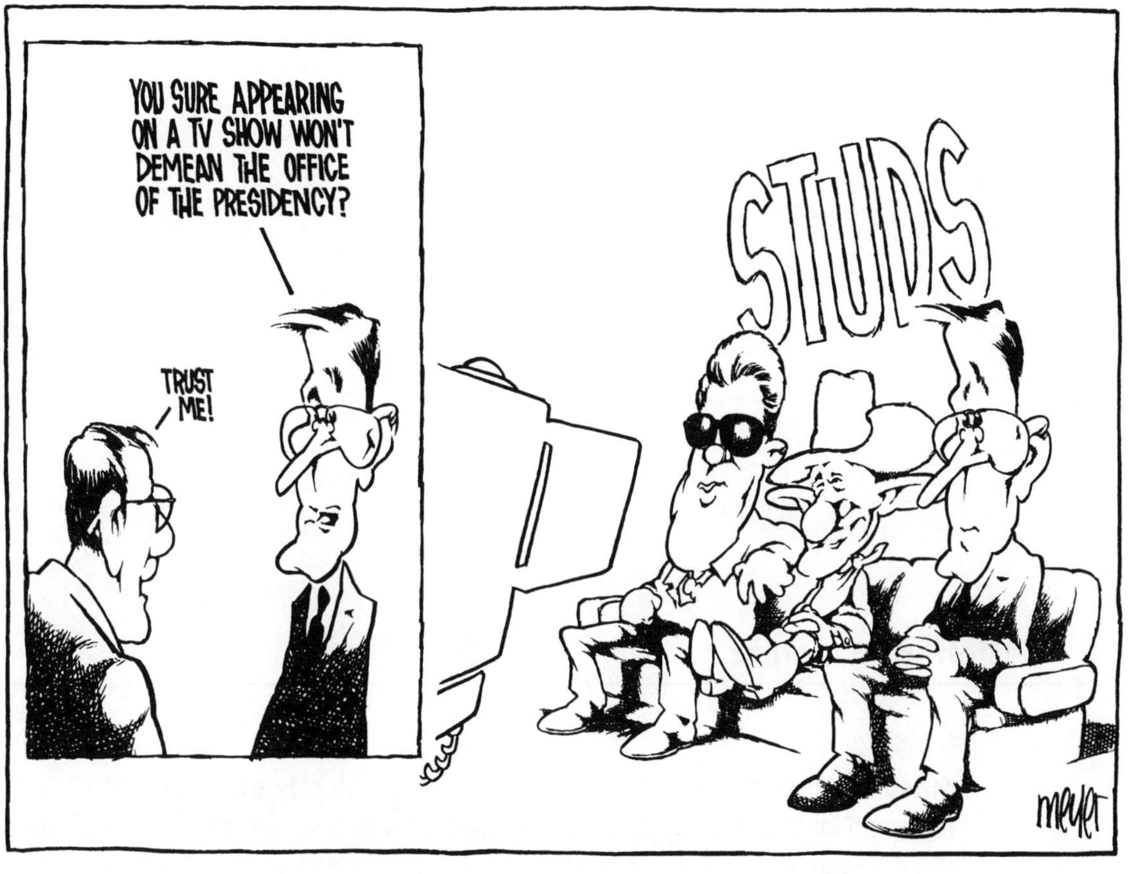
YOU SURE APPEARING ON A TV SHOW WON'T DEMEAN THE OFFICE OF THE PRESIDENCY?
TRUST ME!
STUDS
meyer

Michael Ramirez

Many accused the media of giving Clinton a free ride to the White House. For Clinton supporters, however, it didn't seem that way early in the campaign, when the candidate was hammered on issue after issue.

Courtesy of Michael Ramirez and *The* (Memphis) *Commercial Appeal*

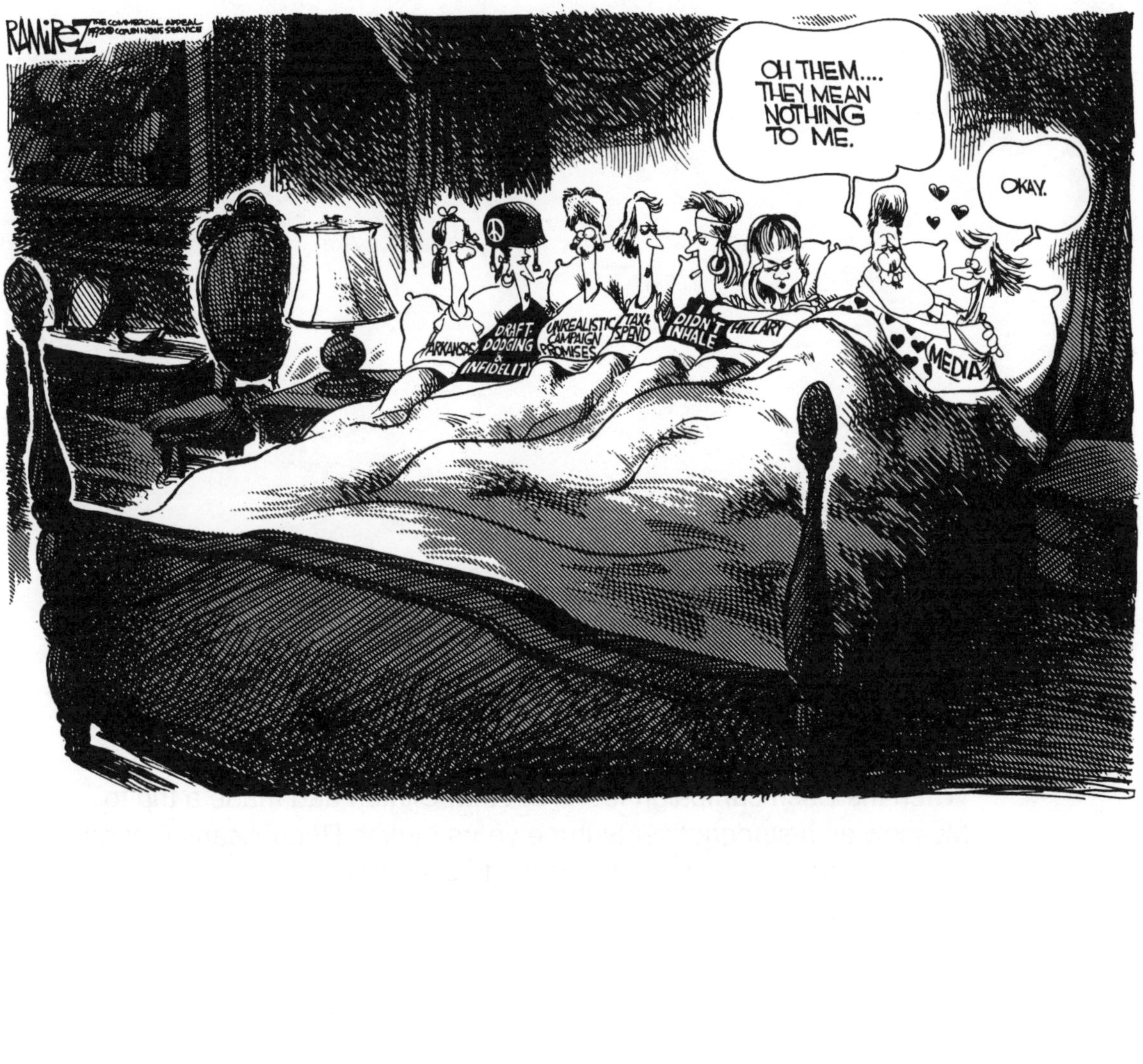
RAMIREZ
ARKANSAS
DRAFT-DODGING & INFIDELITY
UNREALISTIC CAMPAIGN PROMISES
TAX & SPEND
DIDN'T INHALE
HILLARY
OH THEM.... THEY MEAN NOTHING TO ME.
OKAY.
MEDIA

Moscow

Tom Meyer

When the Bush campaign found out that Clinton had made a trip to Moscow as a student twenty-three years earlier, Republicans thought they'd found a new "character" issue to use against the Arkansas governor.

© Tom Meyer, *San Francisco Chronicle*

RECENTLY RELEASED EVIDENCE SUGGESTS CLINTON MAY HAVE BEEN IN MOSCOW BEFORE HIS OXFORD TRIP

Doonesbury

Republicans did their best to dream up a scenario of Clinton's activities during his visit to Moscow.

GOTTA GET SOME SLEEP... GOTTA BE IN... Z-CITY...
UNIVERSAL PRESS SYNDICATE © 1992 G.B. Trudeau
GOTTA... GET... ZZZZ!
HOLD IT! Y'ALL ARE KGB?
TOO LATE, MY LITTLE LOVEBIRD! WE HAVE PHOTOS!
GOT HIM! GOT HIM!
GEORGE, I'M MOVING INTO THE GUEST ROOM.
10-23
GB Trudeau

Chip Bok

Bush went on the "Larry King Show" to suggest that Clinton owed the American people a full accounting of the Moscow trip.

By permission of Chip Bok and Creators Syndicate

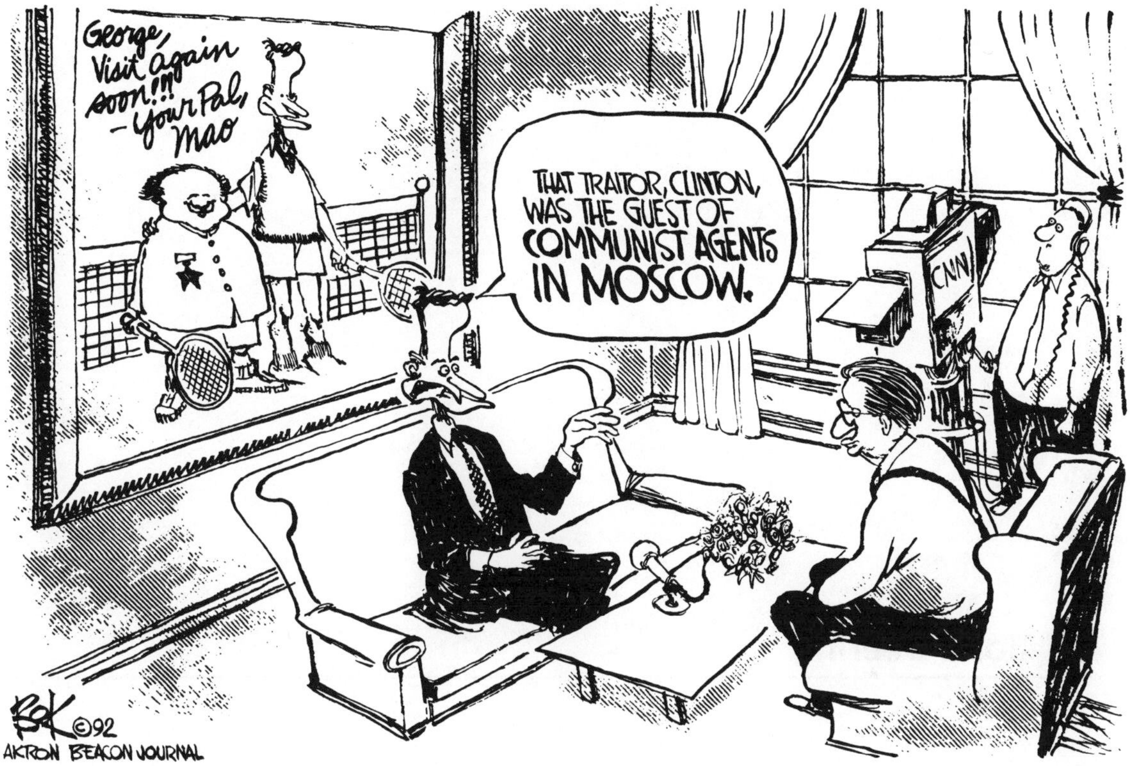
George, Visit again soon!!! - Your Pal, Mao
THAT TRAITOR, CLINTON, WAS THE GUEST OF COMMUNIST AGENTS IN MOSCOW.
CNN
BOK ©92
AKRON BEACON JOURNAL

John Deering

In a last ditch effort to stop the Clinton juggernaut, the State Department searched Clinton's passport files, hoping to find campaign "dirt." Later, it was discovered that the State Department had also searched through the files of Virginia Kelley, Clinton's mother.

Courtesy of John Deering and the *Arkansas Democrat-Gazette*

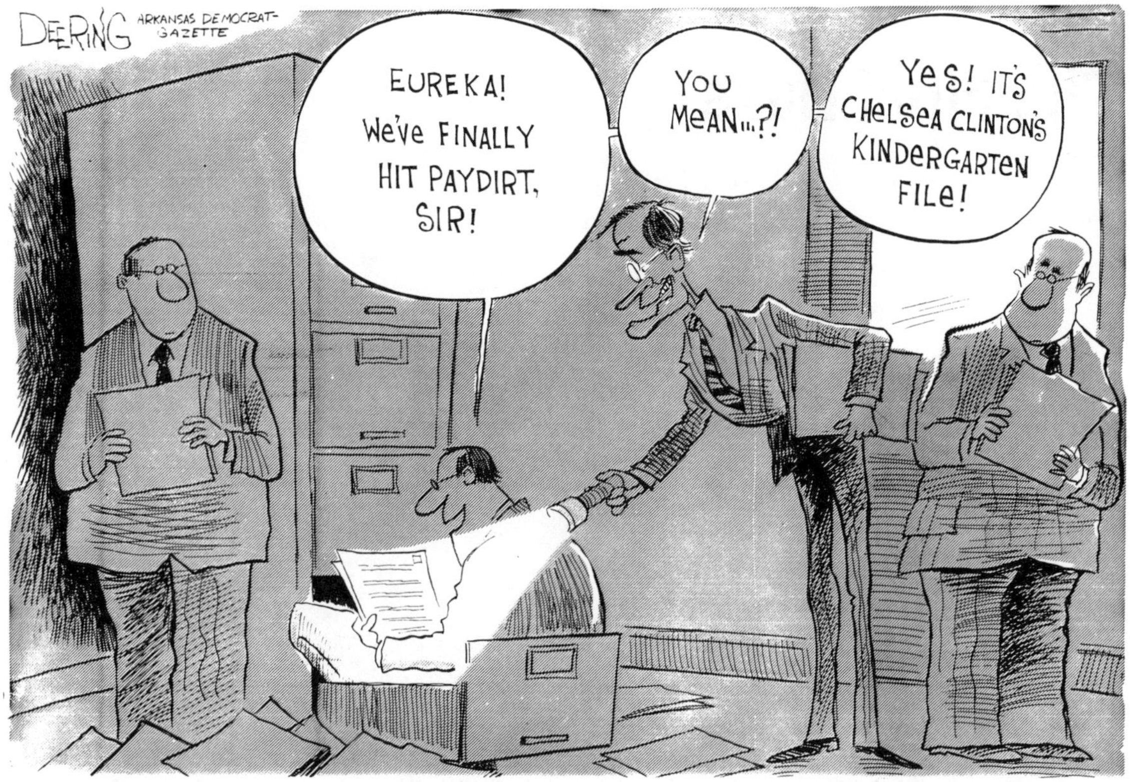
DEERING ARKANSAS DEMOCRAT-GAZETTE
EUREKA! We've FINALLY HIT PAYDIRT, SIR!
YOU MEAN...?!
YeS! IT'S CHELSEA CLINTON'S KINDERGARTEN FILE!

The Final Days

Mike Peters

It didn't look good for the Bush administration when the FBI, the CIA, and the Justice Department decided to investigate each other in the midst of the fall campaign.

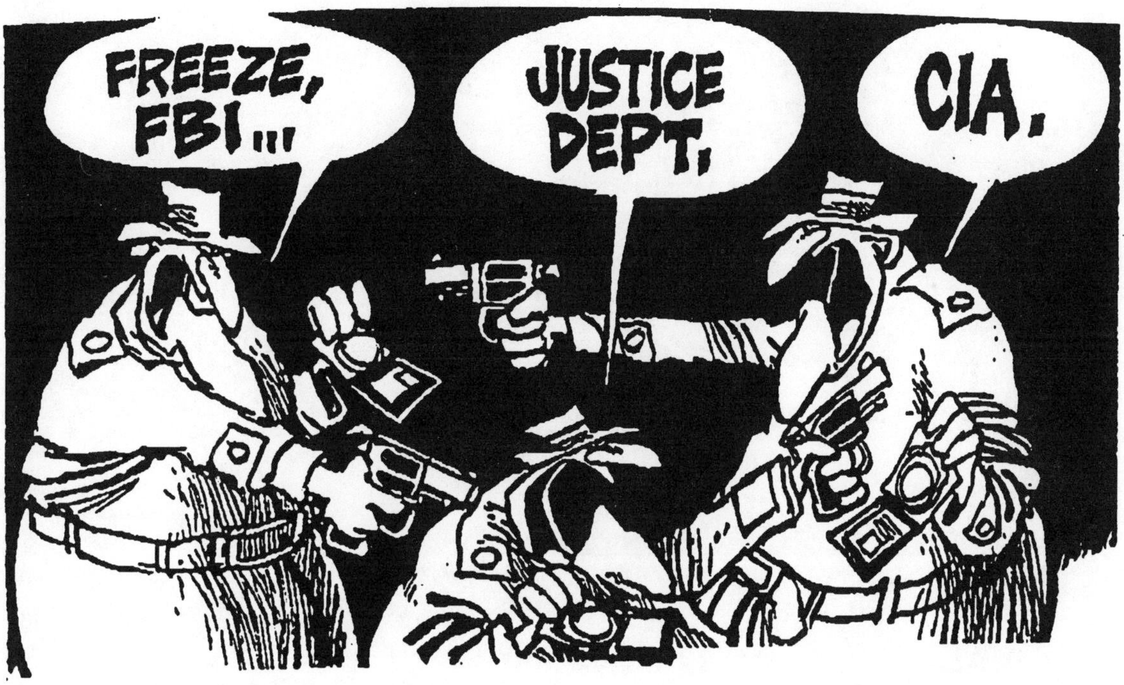
FREEZE, FBI...
JUSTICE DEPT,
CIA.

KAL

For Bush, more than one closet seemed to contain foreign-policy skeletons.

Cartoonists and Writers Syndicate

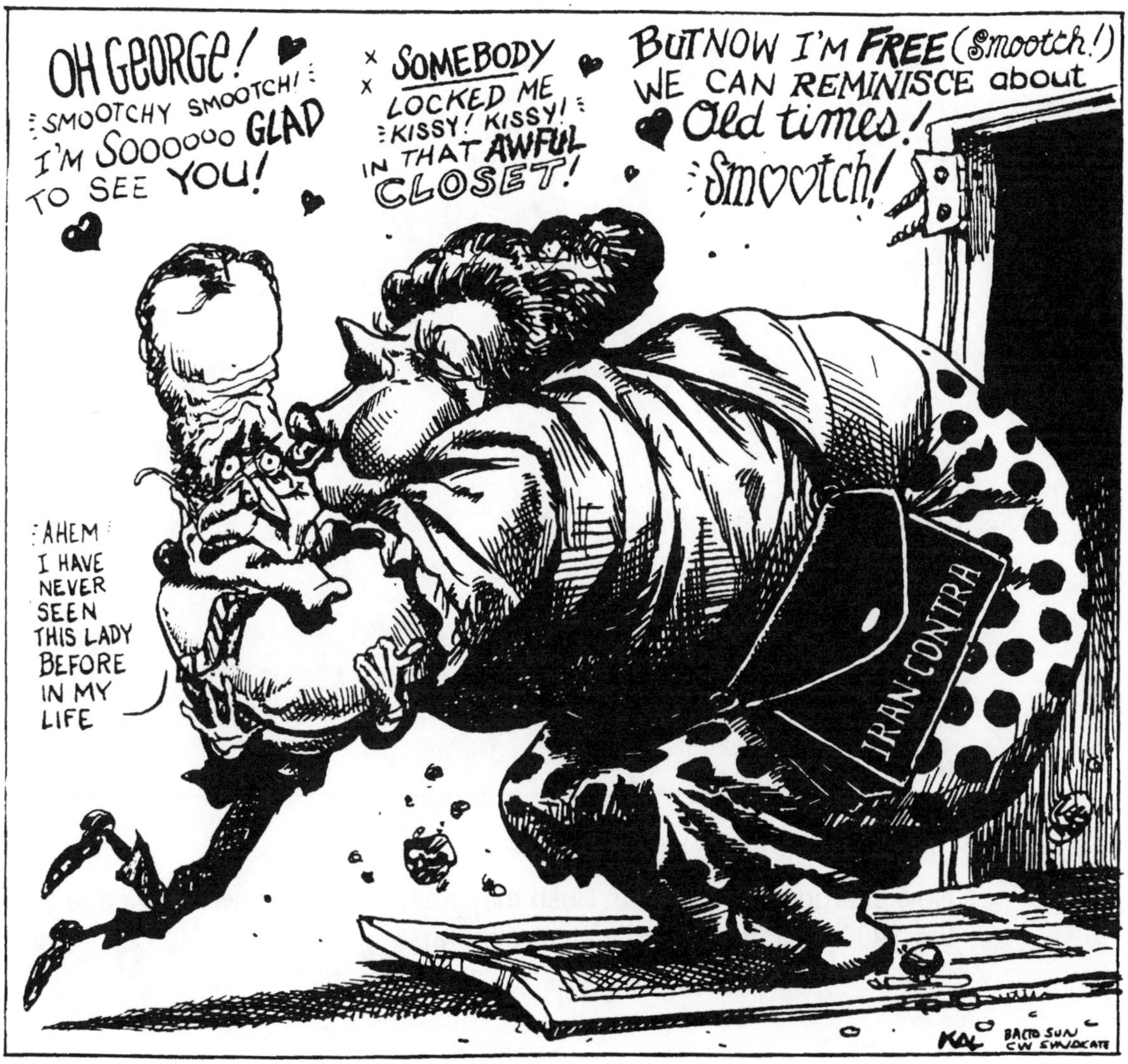
OH GEORGE!
SMOOTCHY SMOOTCH! I'M SOOOOOO GLAD TO SEE YOU!
SOMEBODY LOCKED ME KISSY! KISSY! IN THAT AWFUL CLOSET!
BUT NOW I'M FREE (Smootch!) WE CAN REMINISCE about Old times!
Smootch!
AHEM I HAVE NEVER SEEN THIS LADY BEFORE IN MY LIFE
IRAN-CONTRA
KAL
BALTO SUN CW SYNDICATE

AUTH

New charges emerged that Bush may have lied about his knowledge of the 1986 arms-for-hostages deal with Iran.

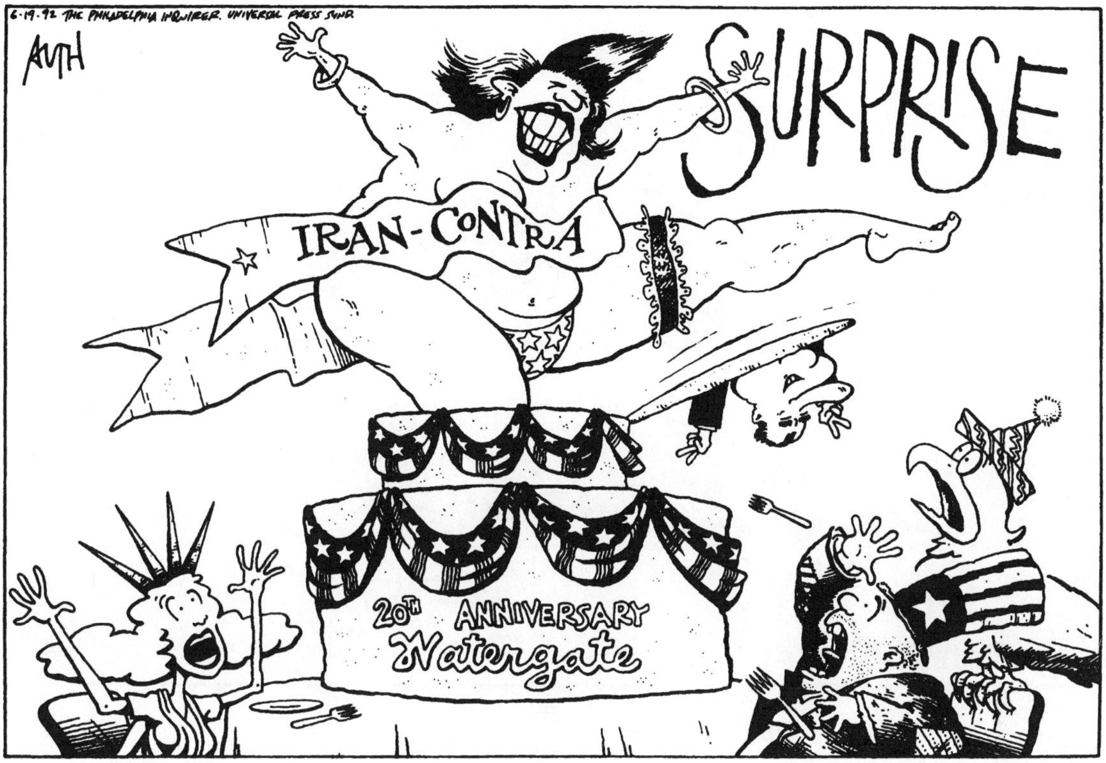
6-19-92 THE PHILADELPHIA INQUIRER. UNIVERSAL PRESS SYND.
AUTH
SURPRISE
IRAN-CONTRA
20TH ANNIVERSARY
Watergate

Dan Foote

As the election neared, domestic issues continued to favor the Democrats and Clinton.

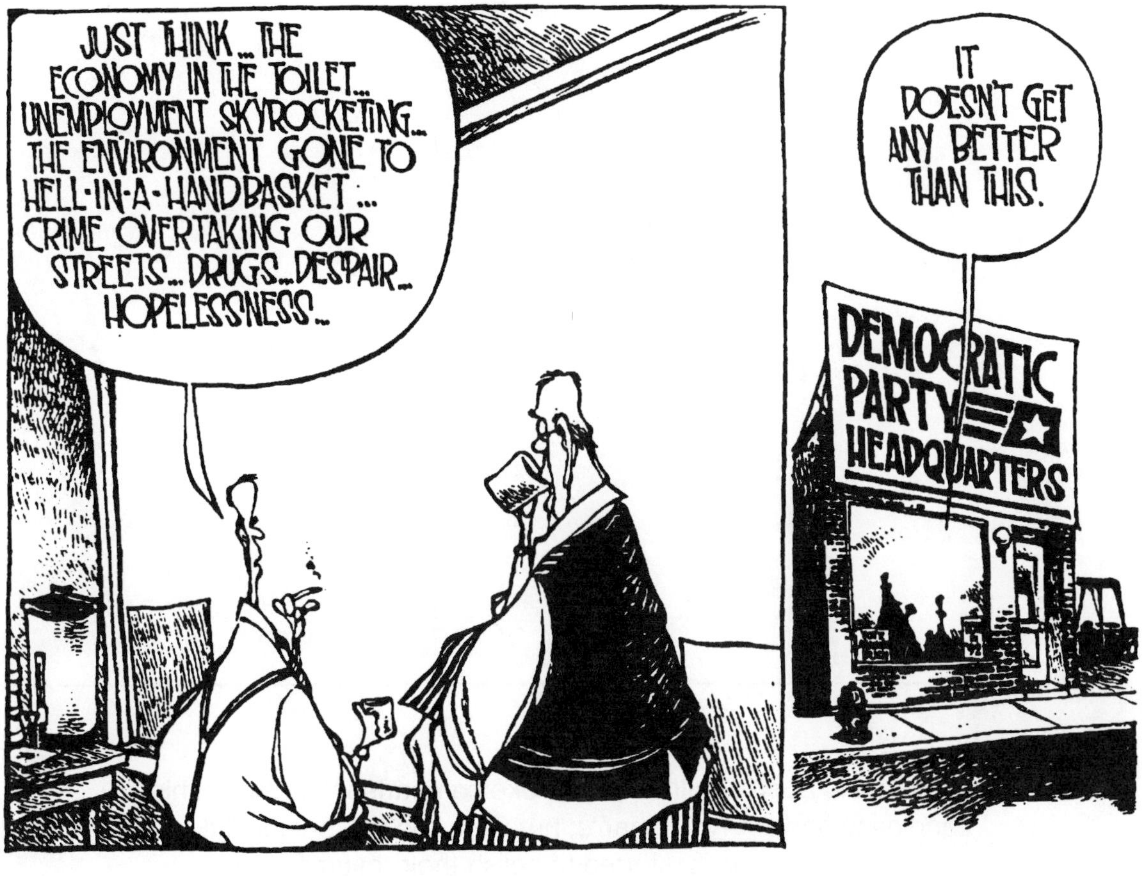
JUST THINK...THE ECONOMY IN THE TOILET... UNEMPLOYMENT SKYROCKETING... THE ENVIRONMENT GONE TO HELL-IN-A-HANDBASKET... CRIME OVERTAKING OUR STREETS...DRUGS...DESPAIR... HOPELESSNESS...
IT DOESN'T GET ANY BETTER THAN THIS.
DEMOCRATIC PARTY HEADQUARTERS

Jeff MacNelly

To no avail, Bush continued to invoke comparisons between his candidacy and Harry Truman's; but Republicans, seeing little movement in the polls, started to polish their résumés.

Reprinted by permission: Tribune Media Services

MACNELLY Chicago Tribune.
GIVE 'EM HELL, MR. PRESIDENT!
RÉSUMÉ

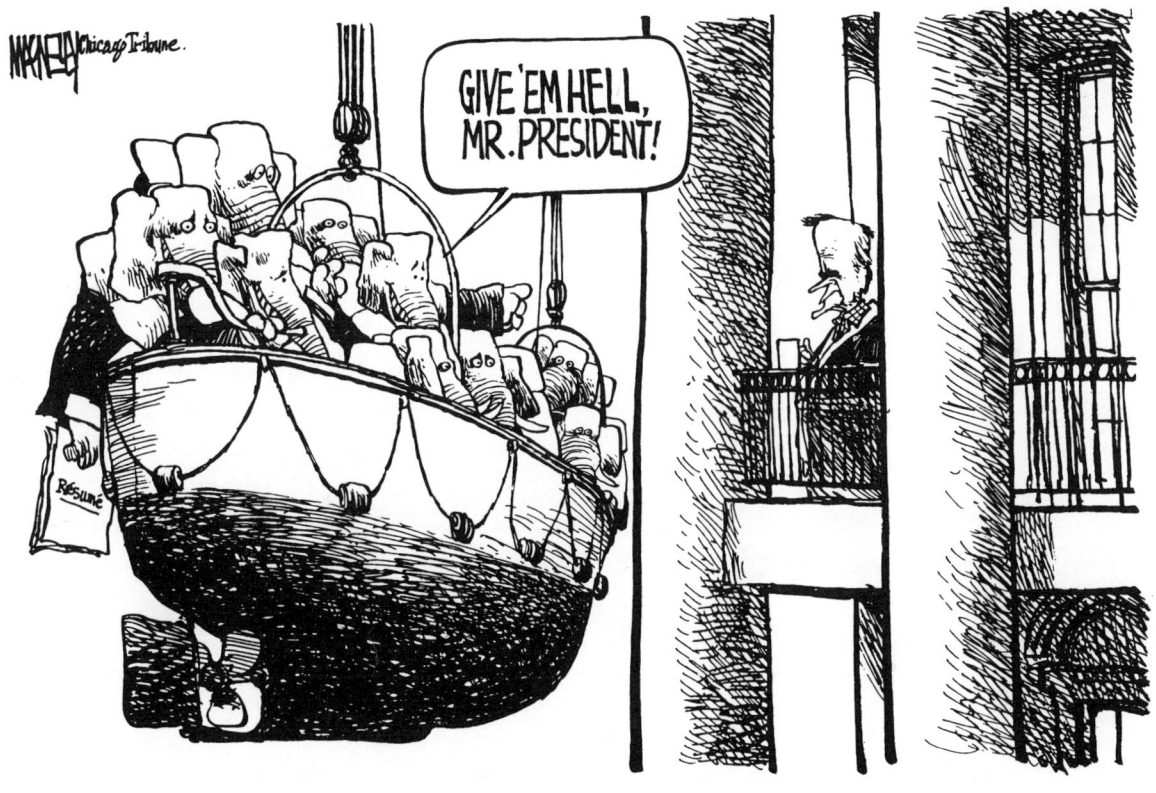

Mike Peters

As Clinton fought exhaustion from his self-imposed, marathon-like campaign schedule, he often had problems keeping his voice.

BY MIKE PETERS FOR THE DAYTON DAILY NEWS

QUICK...GOVERNOR CLINTON LOST HIS VOICE...IS THERE A **SPIN DOCTOR** IN THE HOUSE?

Dick Wright

Hillary Clinton, at the center of some early campaign controversies, kept what some considered to be a low profile during the remainder of the campaign and down to the last days until the election.

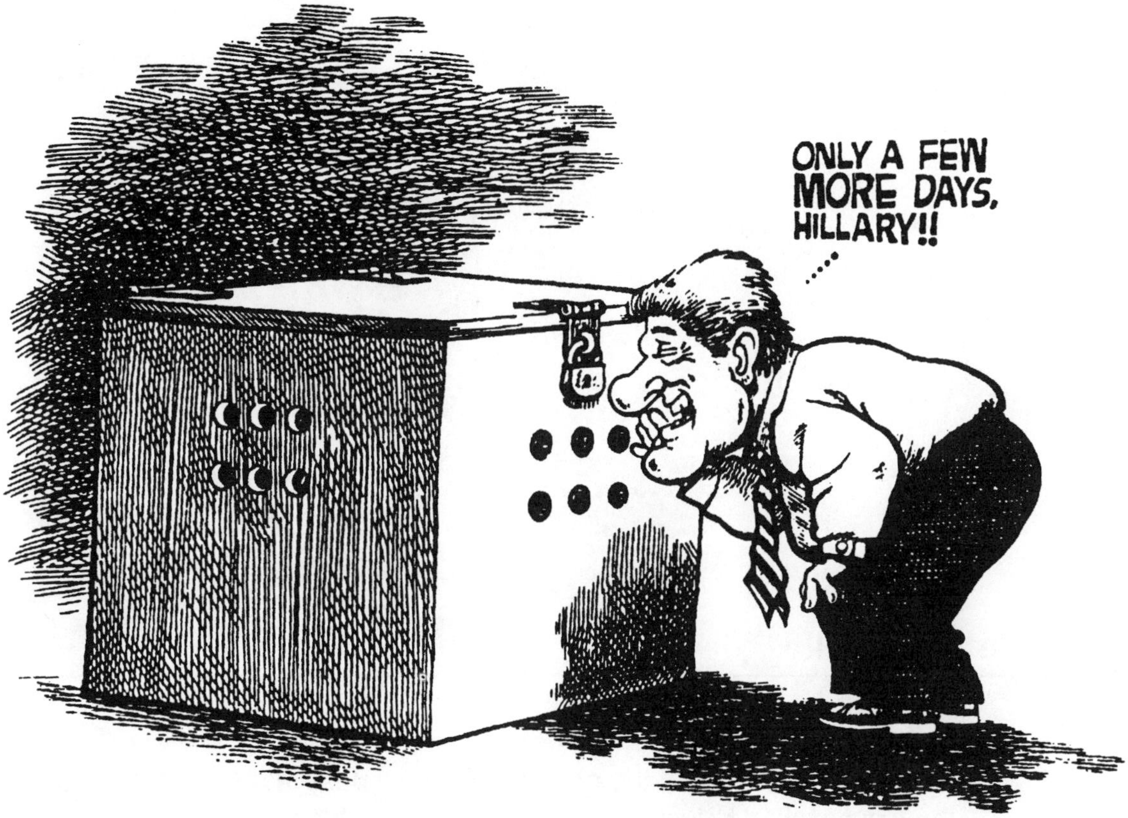
ONLY A FEW MORE DAYS, HILLARY!!

Jeff MacNelly

As it became clear that the presidency would pass into Clinton's hands, the focus shifted to just how well he would be able to govern.

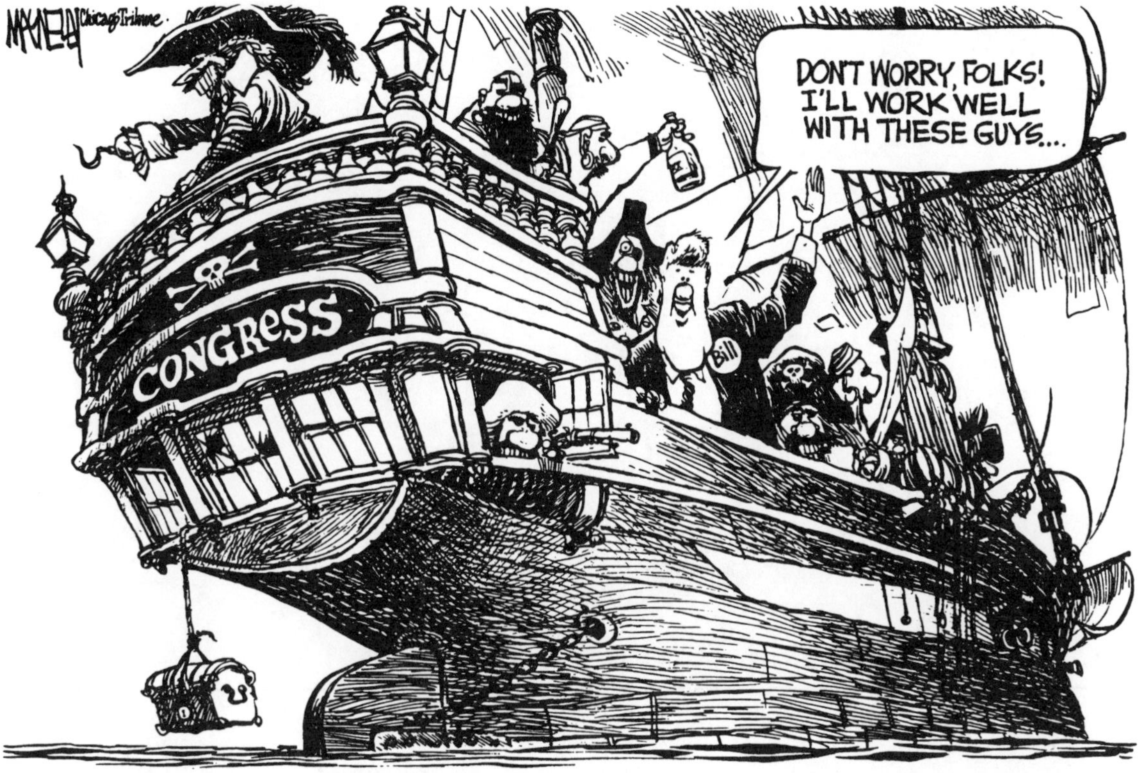
MacNelly Chicago Tribune
DON'T WORRY, FOLKS! I'LL WORK WELL WITH THESE GUYS...
CONGRESS
Bill

Mike Luckovich

As Election Day neared, pollsters began to predict an overwhelming victory for the Arkansas governor in the electoral college. Clinton would go on to capture several states that were part of the Republican victory formula in the past.

Creators Syndicate

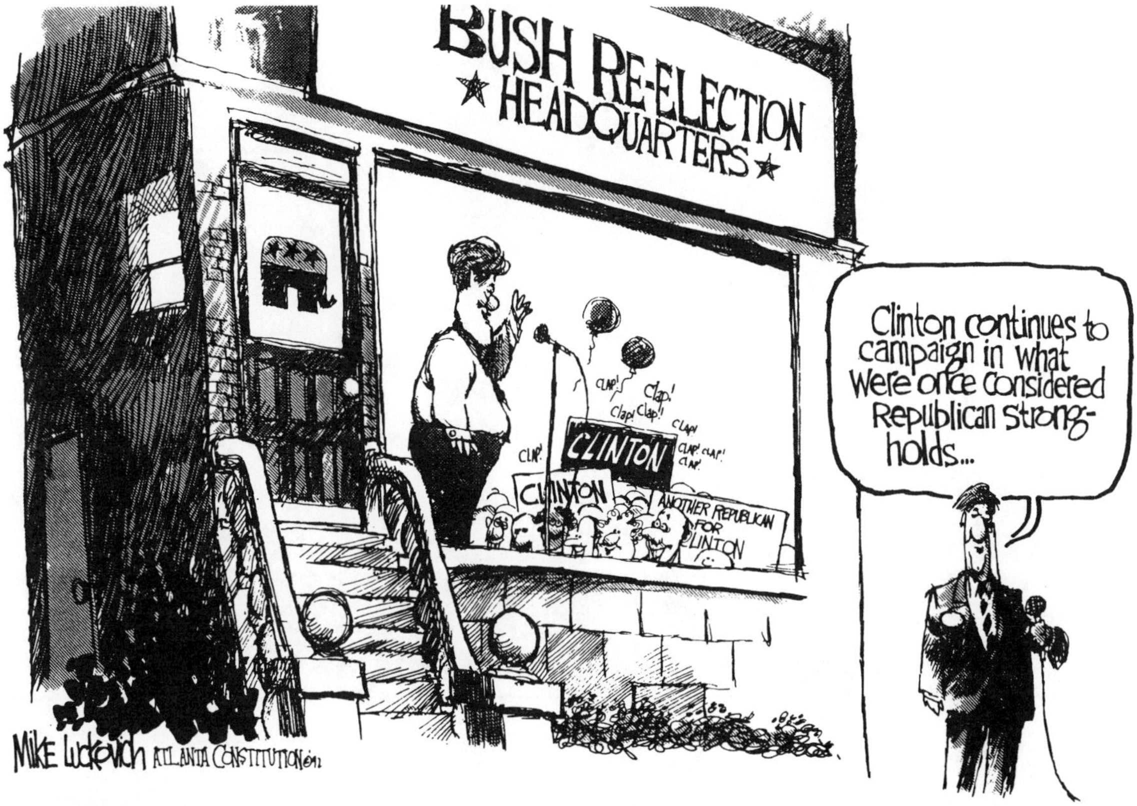
BUSH RE-ELECTION
HEADQUARTERS
CLINTON
CLINTON
ANOTHER REPUBLICAN FOR CLINTON
Clinton continues to campaign in what were once considered Republican strongholds...
MIKE LUCKOVICH ATLANTA CONSTITUTION

David Seavey

For the Clinton campaign, the encouraging poll results had a pressure all their own. Clinton was accused by some of playing it safe and reverting to a bland campaign style as November 3 drew near.

For *USA Today*. Courtesy of David Seavey and *USA Today*

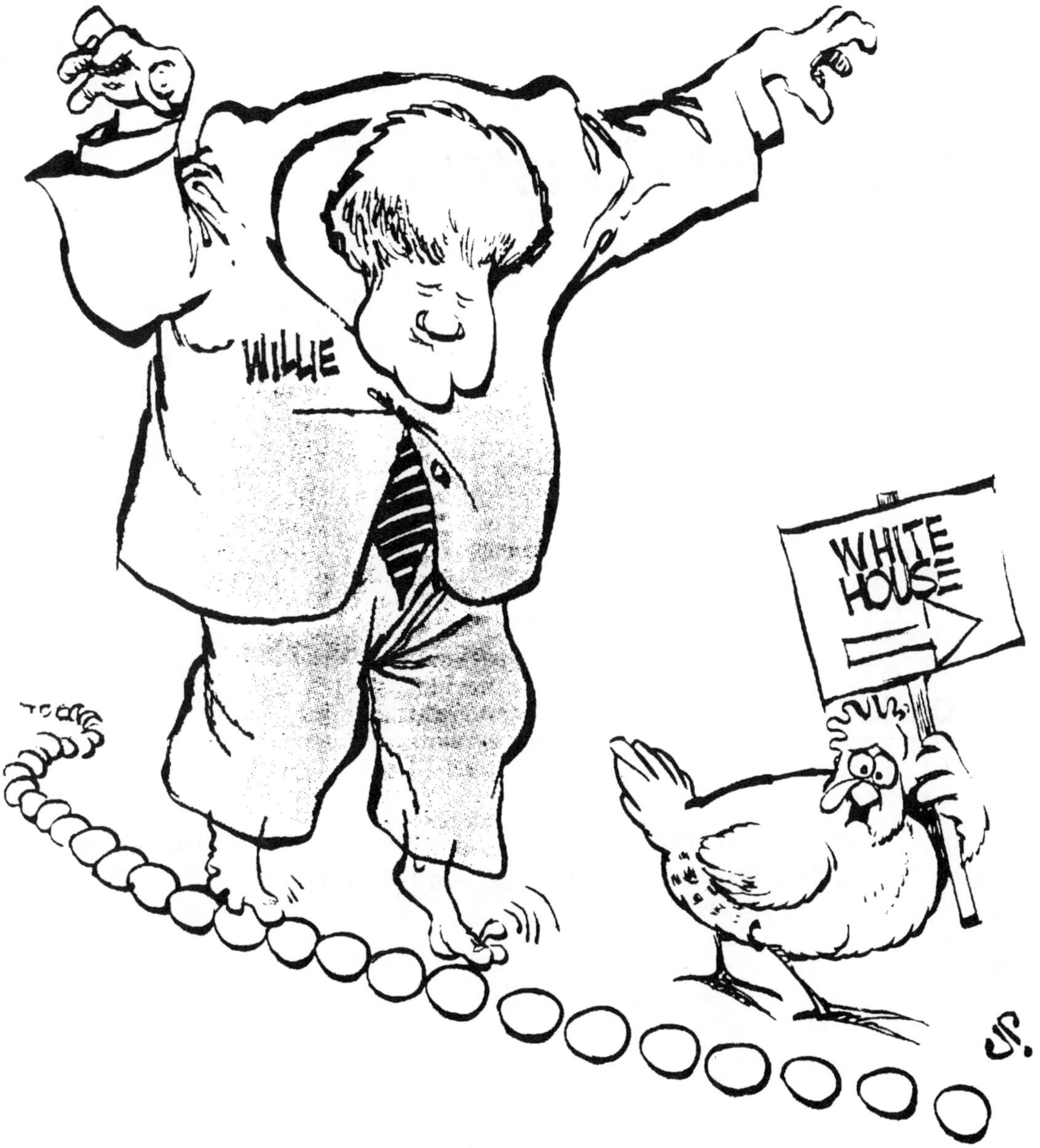
WILLIE
WHITE HOUSE

Easy does it

And the Rest Is History

David Catrow

When election results came in, Arkansas's saxophone-playing governor had plenty of reason to blow his own horn.

Copley News Service

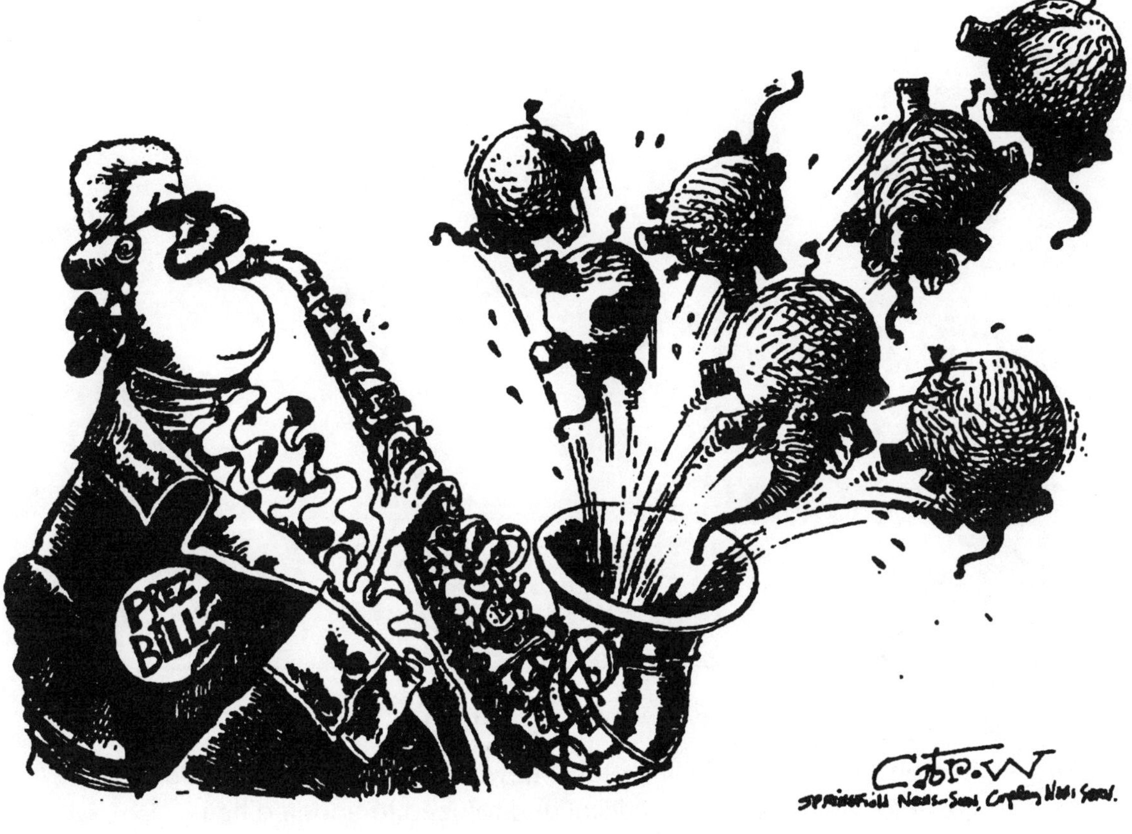
PREZ BILL
SPRINGFIELD NEWS-SUN, COPLEY NEWS SERV.

George Fisher

Clinton had to fight his hometown newspaper, the *Arkansas Democrat-Gazette,* which remained critical and refused to endorse him.

Courtesy of George Fisher and *Arkansas Times*

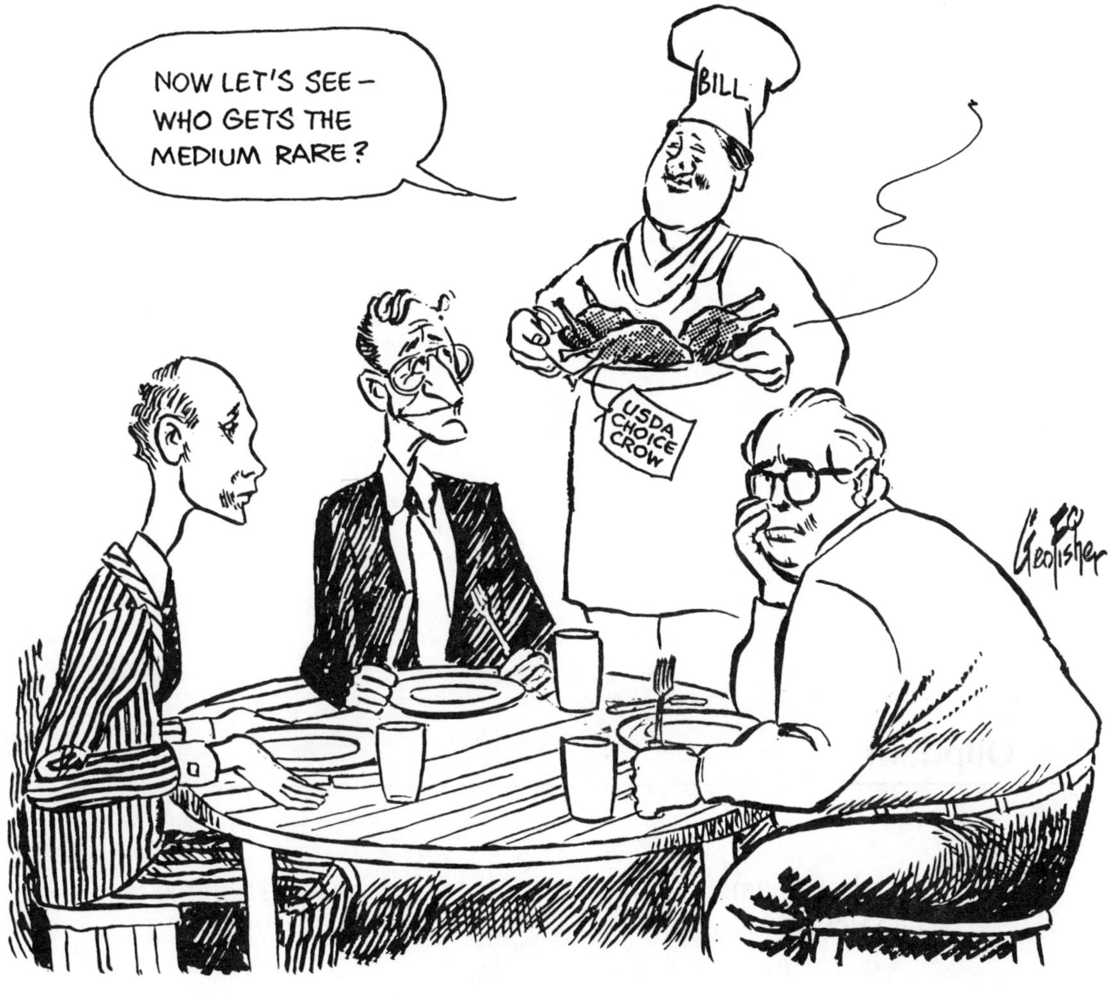
NOW LET'S SEE –
WHO GETS THE
MEDIUM RARE?
BILL
USDA CHOICE CROW
GeoFisher

Oliphant

November 3 came, Clinton won, and Arkansans were headed to the
White House.

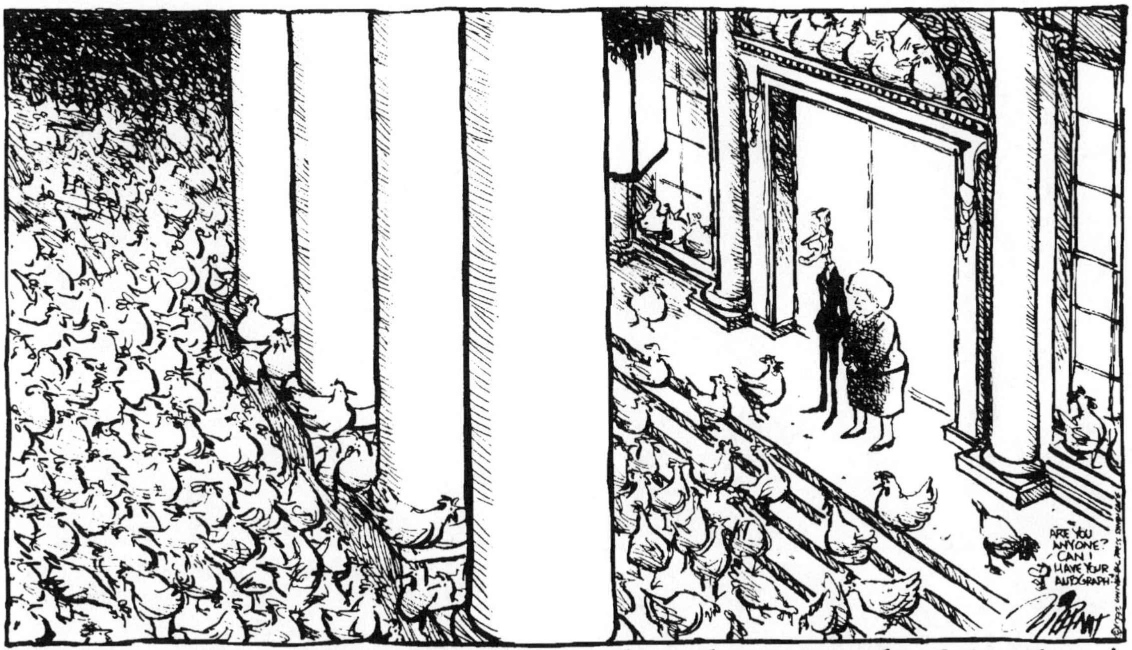
"ARE YOU ANYONE? CAN I HAVE YOUR AUTOGRAPH?"

'EITHER ALL OUR CHICKENS CAME HOME TO ROOST, OR THIS IS THE ARKANSAS TRANSITION TEAM.'

Edward Sorel

If Clinton thought he lived in a fishbowl as governor of Arkansas, moving to Washington threatened to teach him the true meaning of pack journalism.

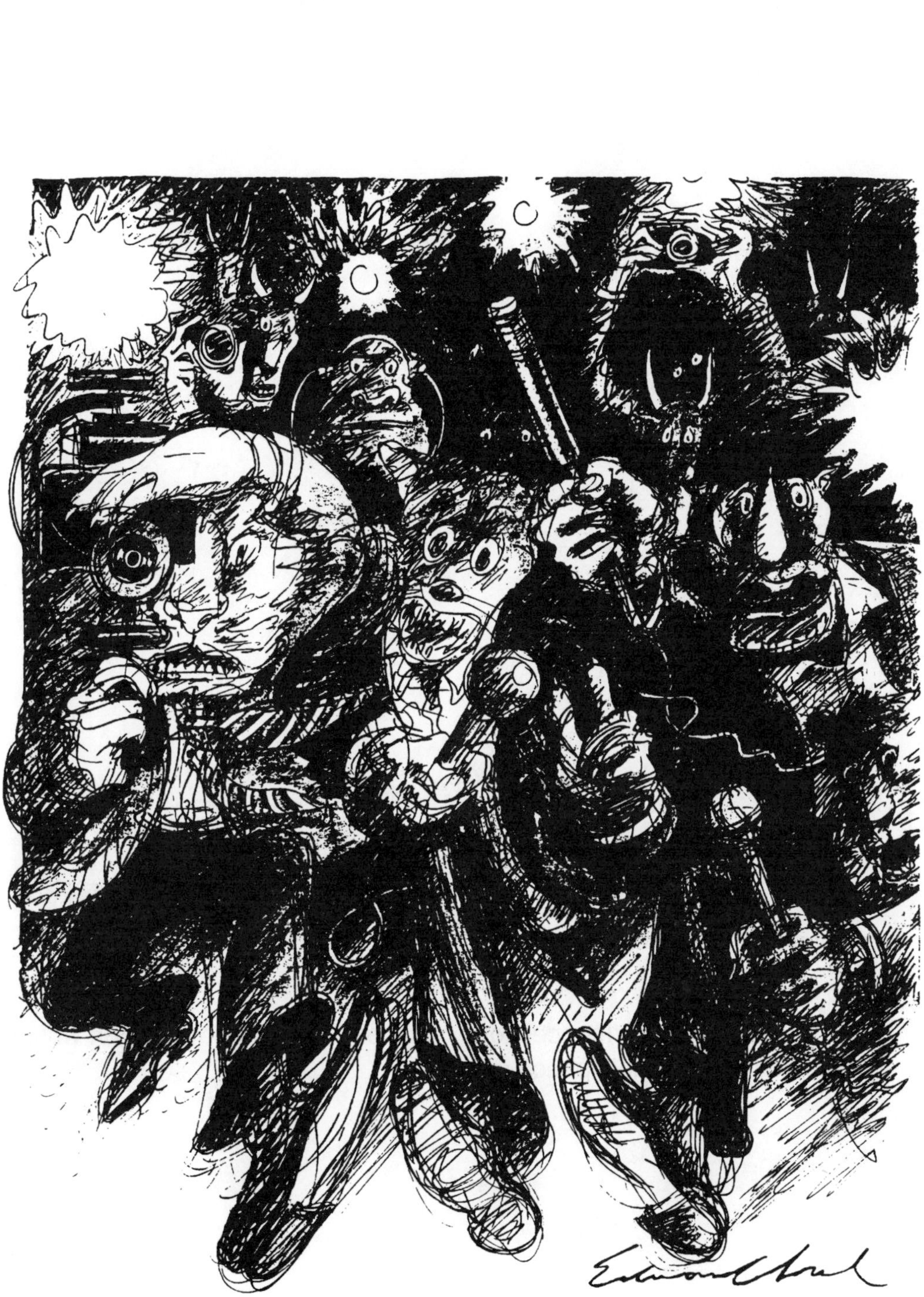

Tom Toles

Given past performances, one could only wonder how Clinton would do in his presidential speech making.

Tom Toles in *The Buffalo News*

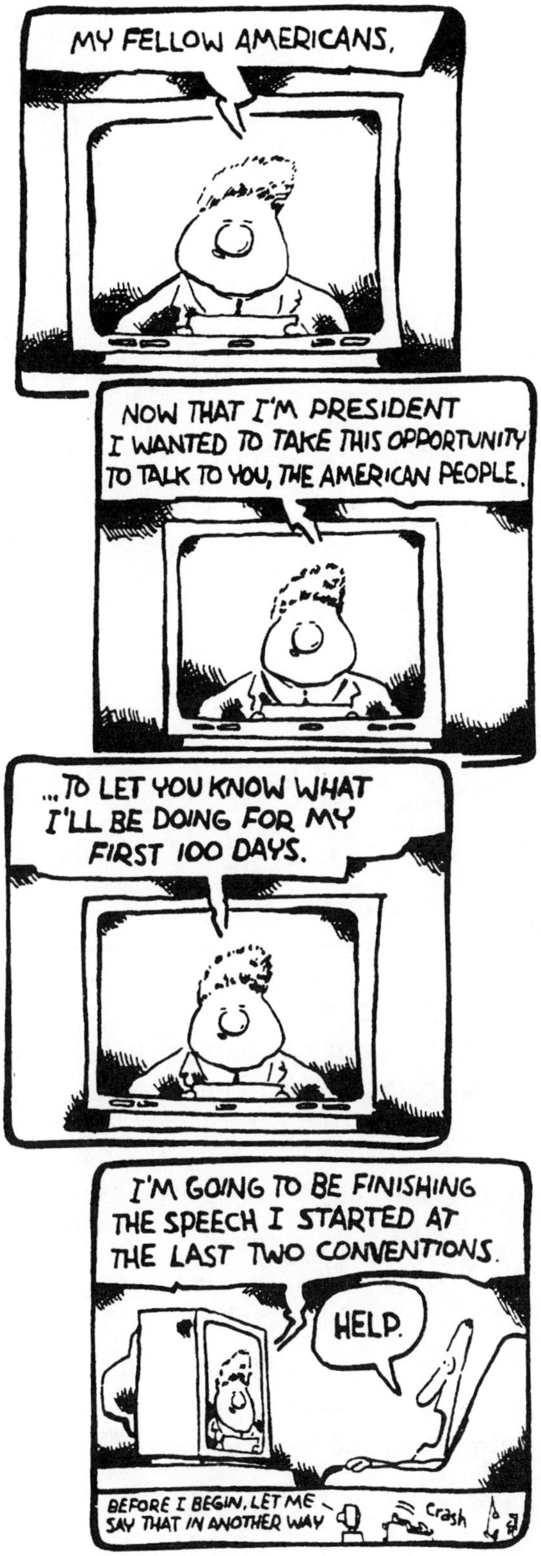
MY FELLOW AMERICANS,
NOW THAT I'M PRESIDENT I WANTED TO TAKE THIS OPPORTUNITY TO TALK TO YOU, THE AMERICAN PEOPLE.
...TO LET YOU KNOW WHAT I'LL BE DOING FOR MY FIRST 100 DAYS.
I'M GOING TO BE FINISHING THE SPEECH I STARTED AT THE LAST TWO CONVENTIONS.
HELP.
BEFORE I BEGIN, LET ME SAY THAT IN ANOTHER WAY
Crash

George Fisher

With a truckload of campaign promises to fulfill, the newly victorious
candidate from Arkansas was ready to set up shop in the White House.

Courtesy of George Fisher and *Arkansas Times*

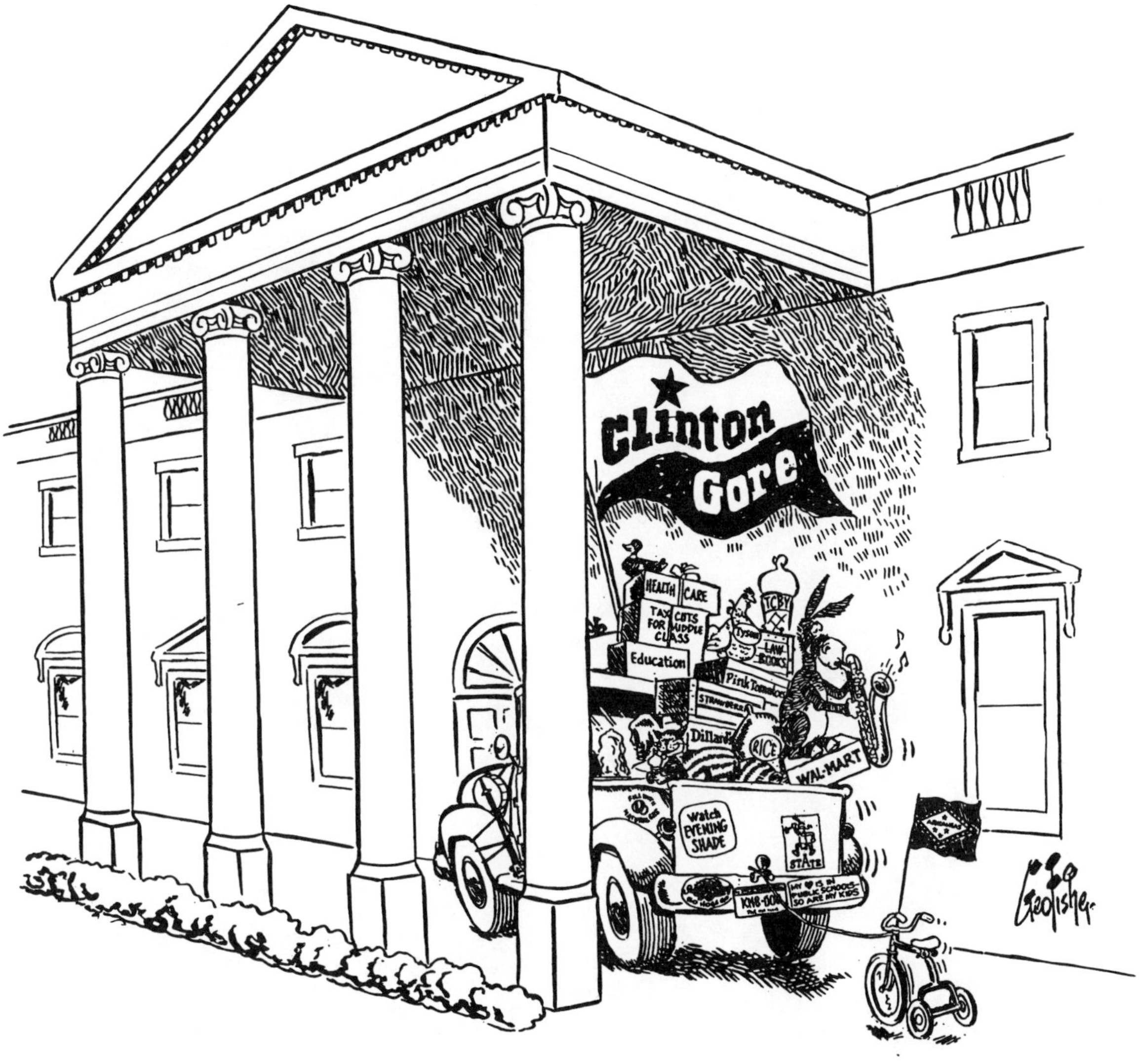
Clinton
Gore
HEALTH CARE
TAX CUTS FOR MIDDLE CLASS
Education
LAW BOOKS
Dillard's
RICE
WAL-MART
Watch EVENING SHADE
STATE